T0066035

THE GOONIES™

THE OFFICIAL COLORING BOOK

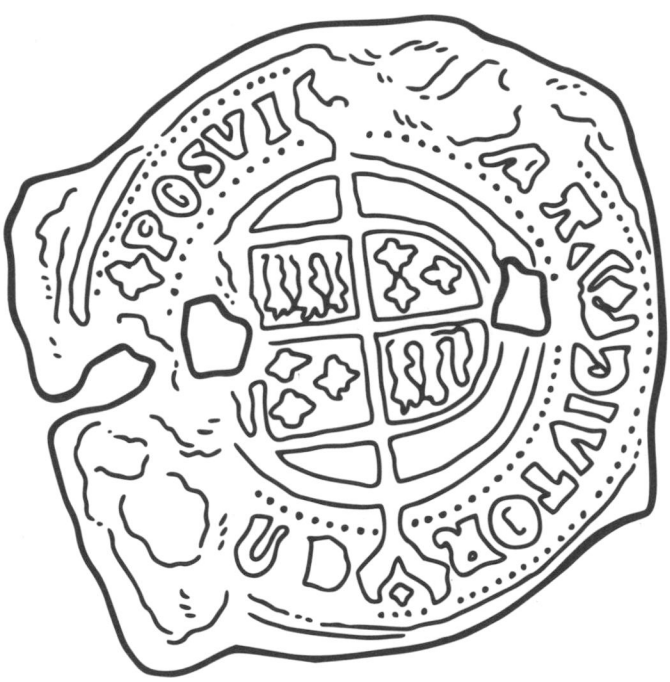

Illustrations by **VALENTIN RAMON**

INSIGHT EDITIONS

SAN RAFAEL • LOS ANGELES • LONDON

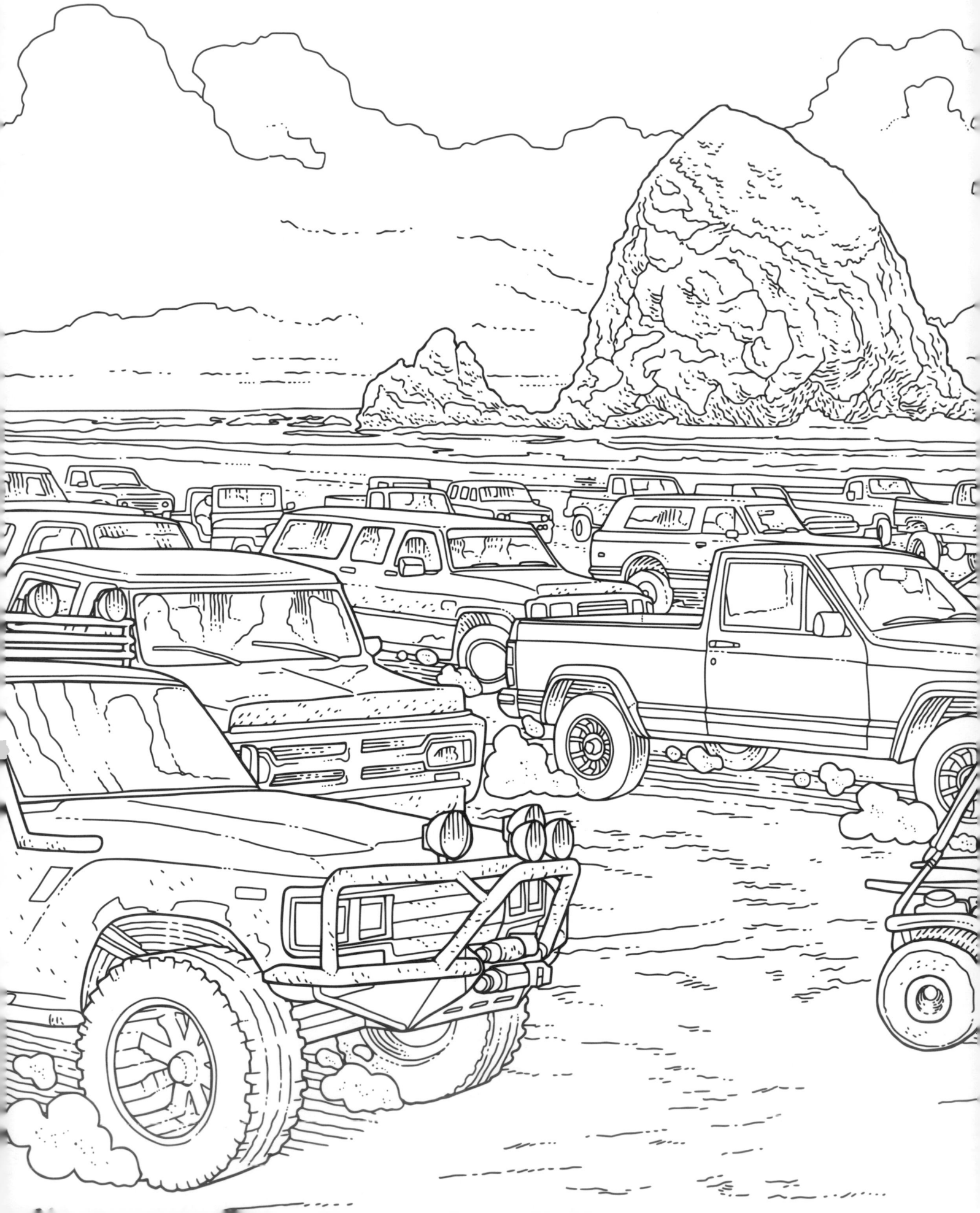

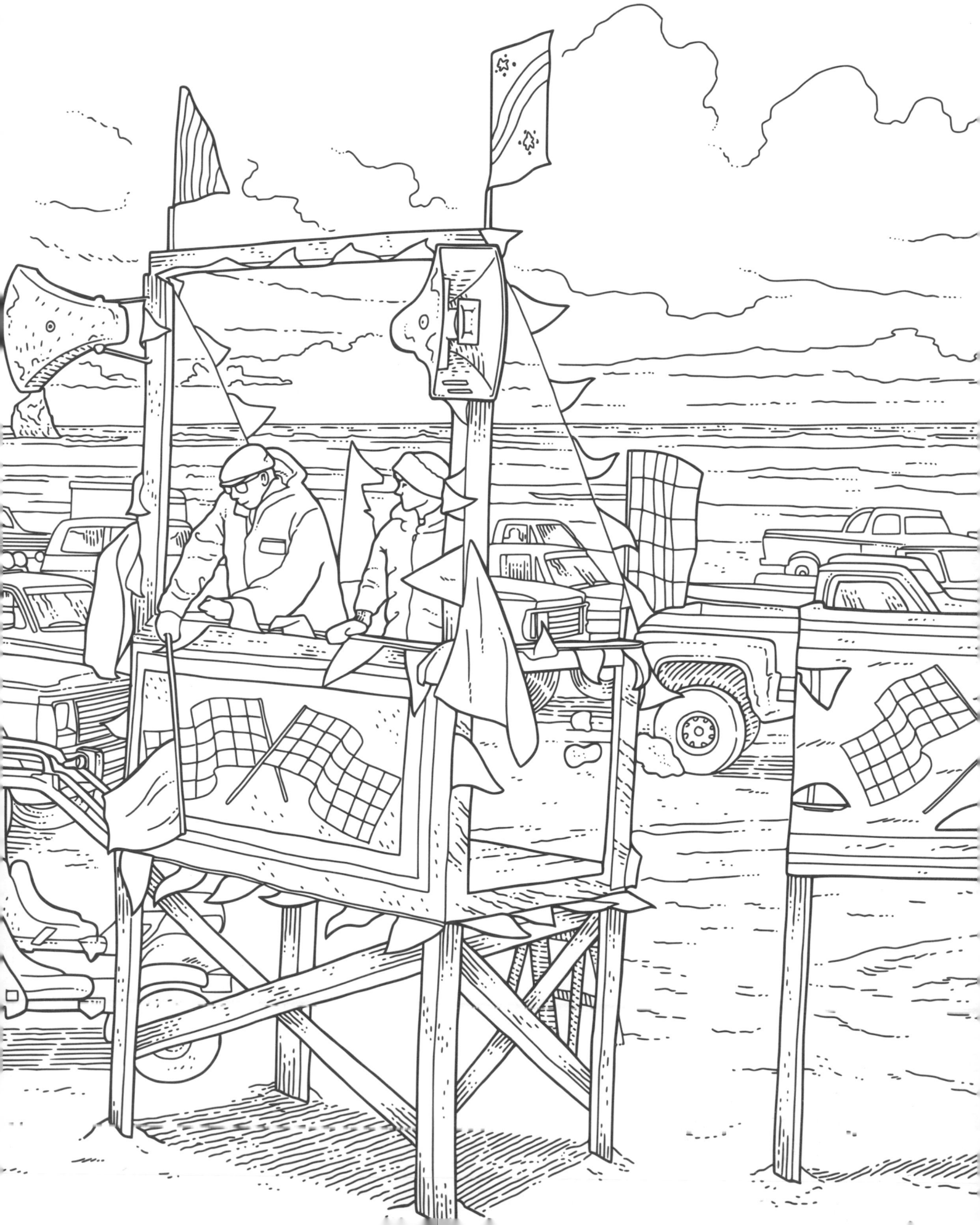

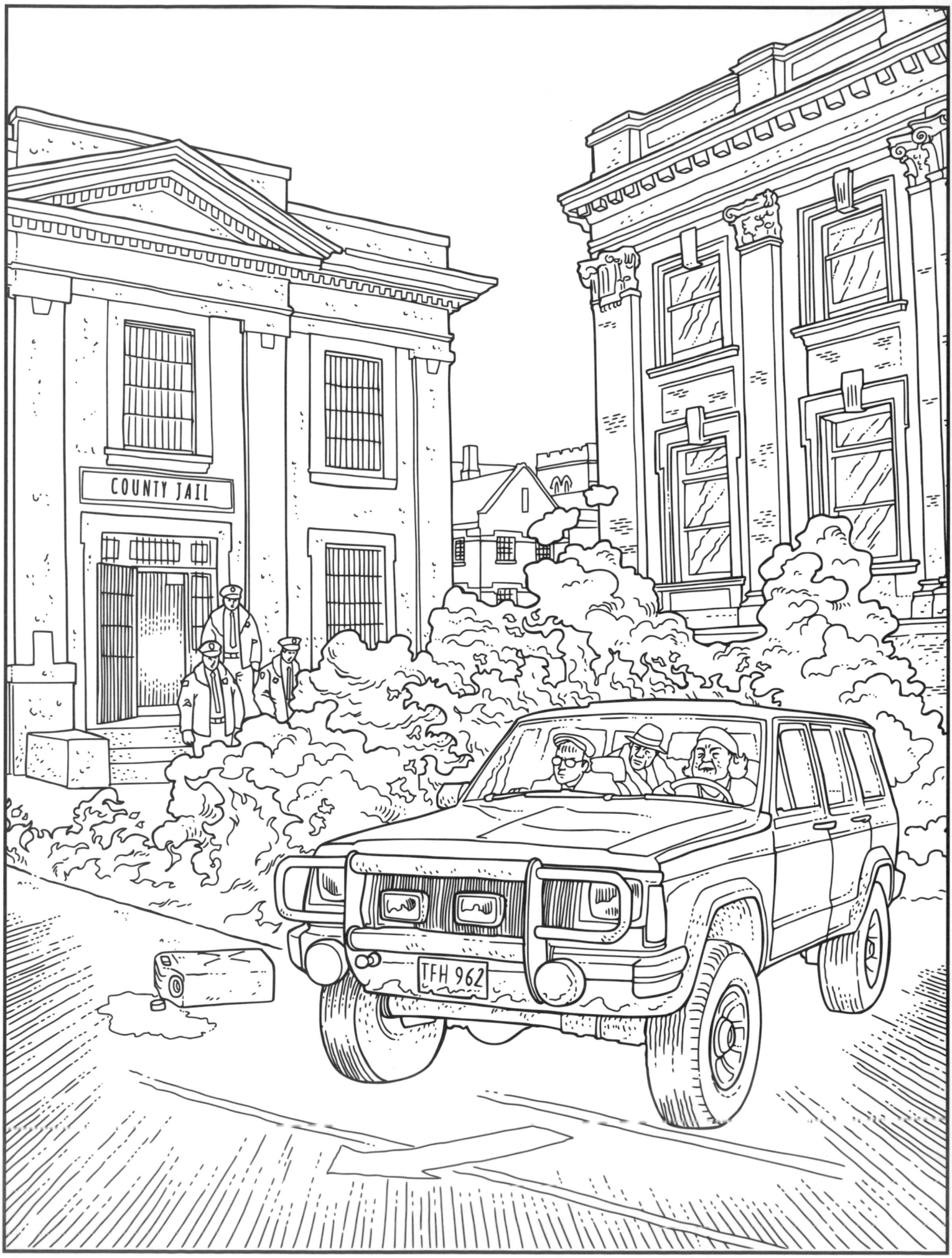
COUNTY JAIL
TFH 962

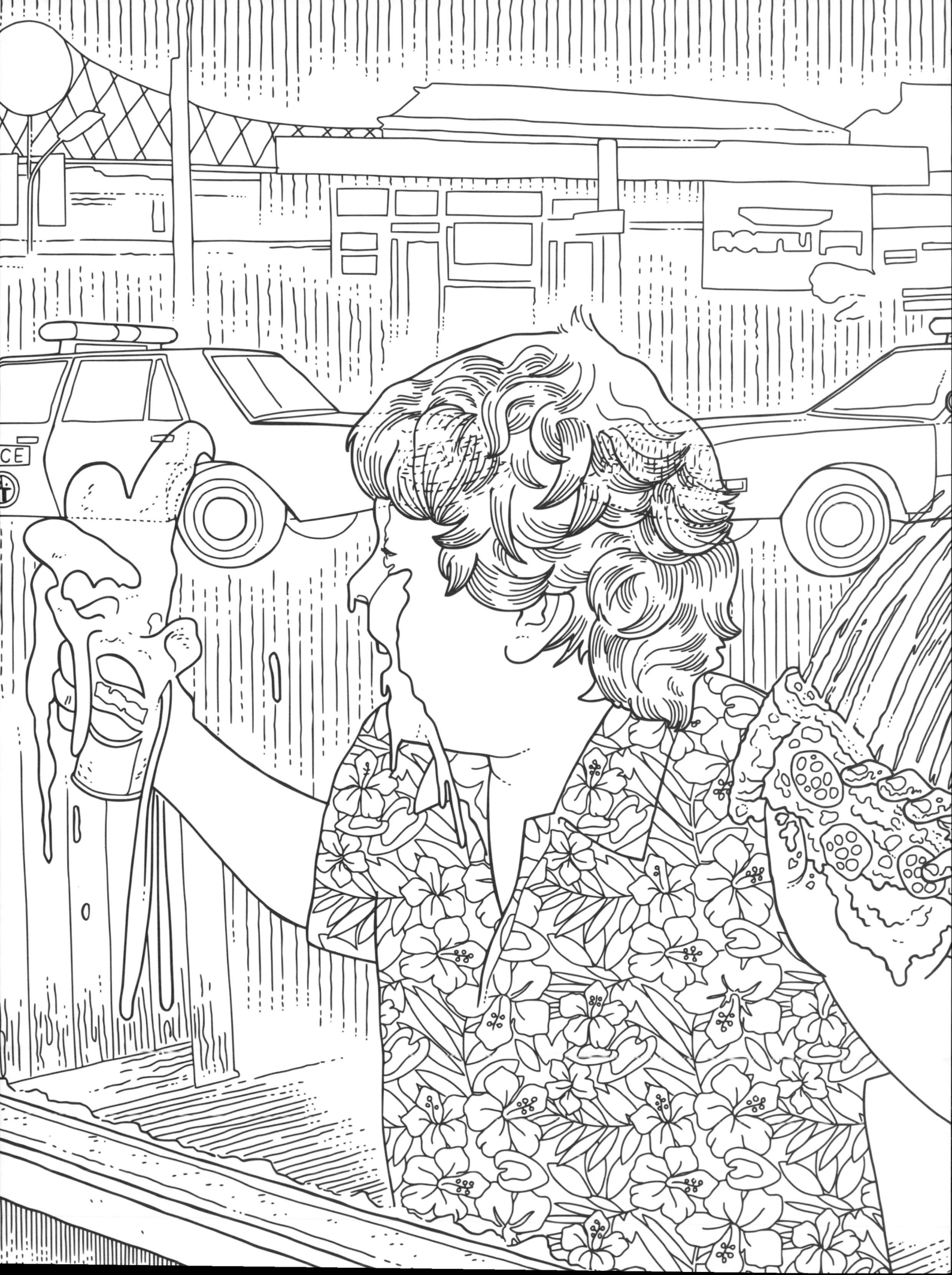
CE

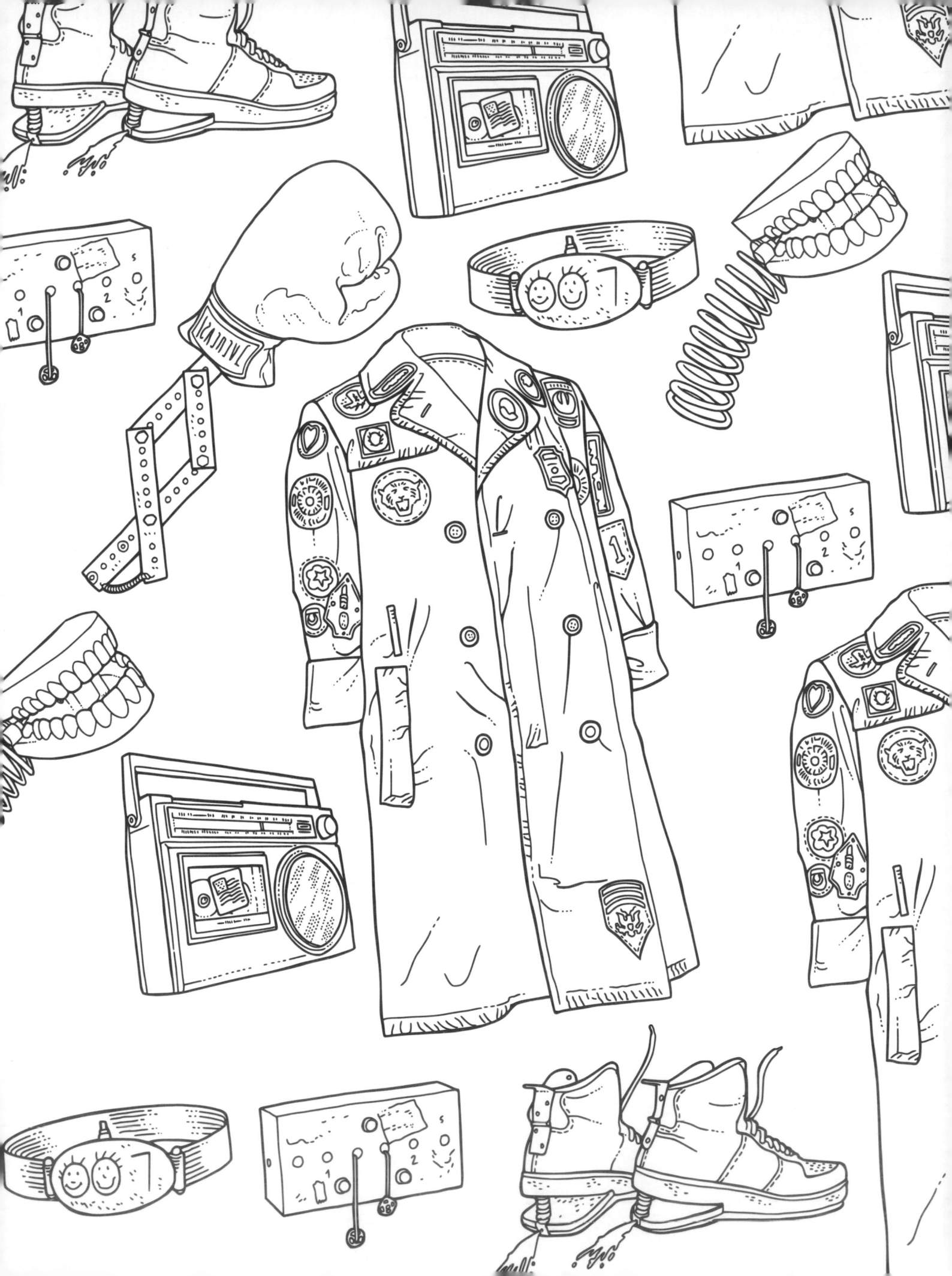

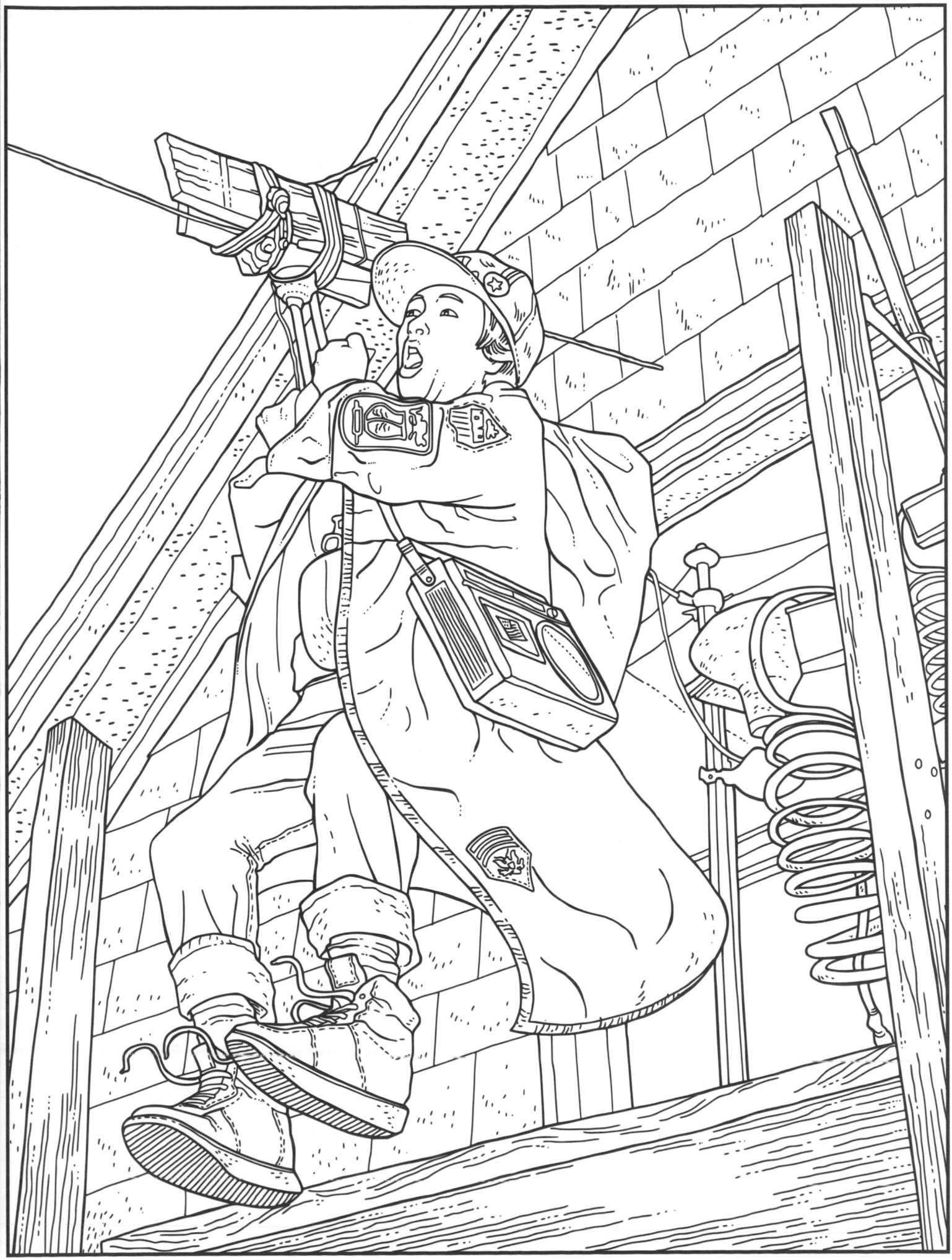

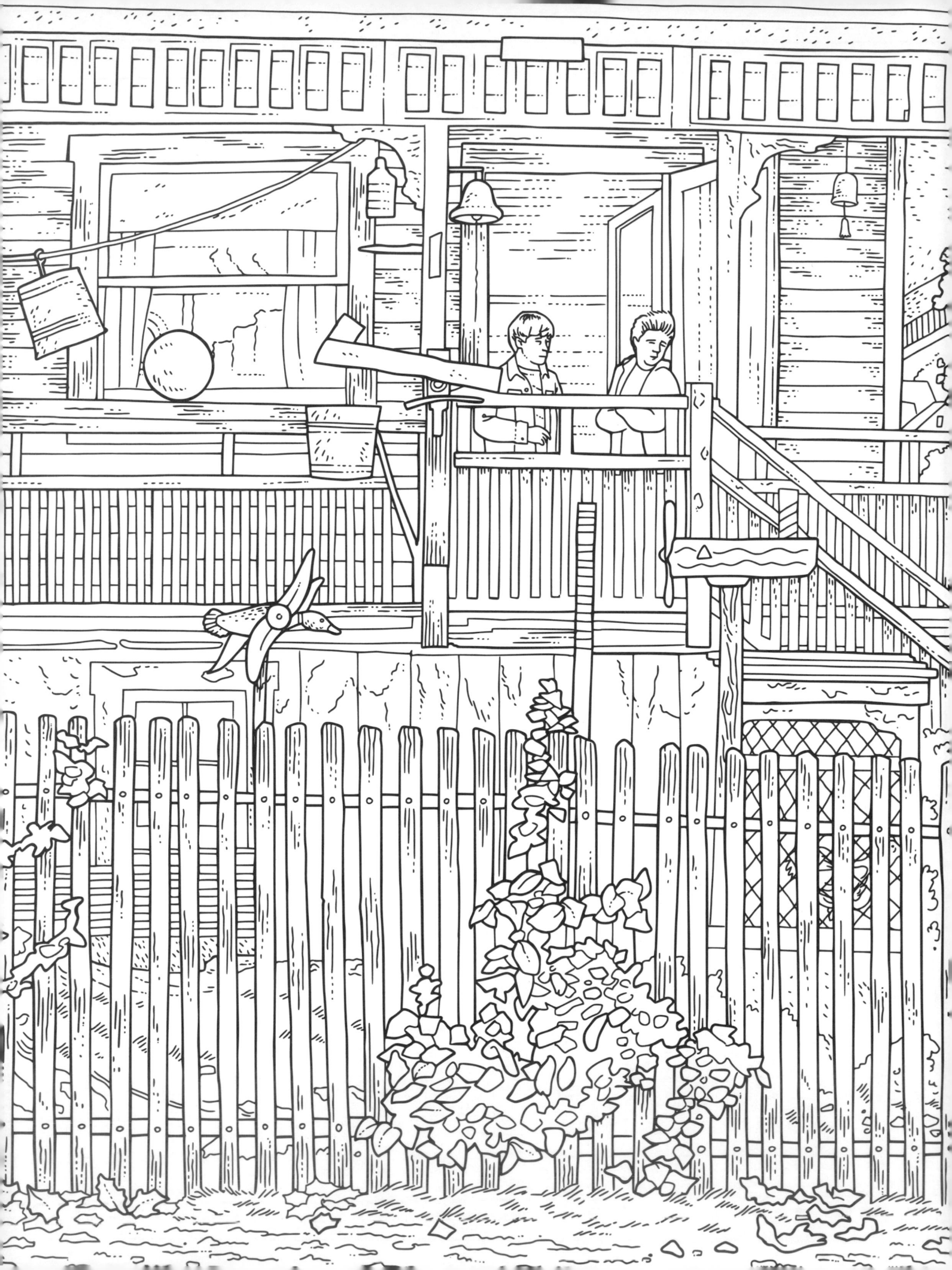

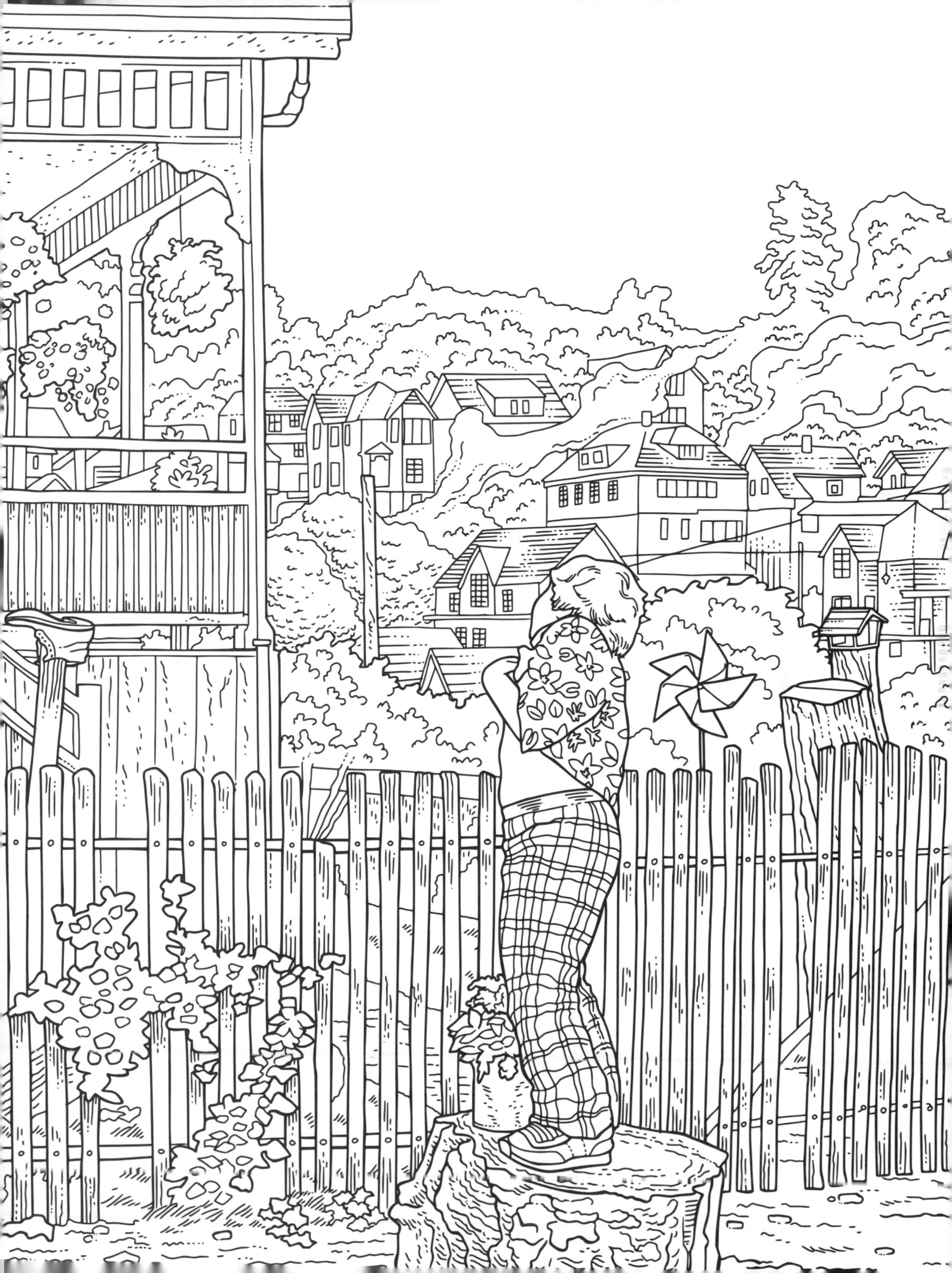

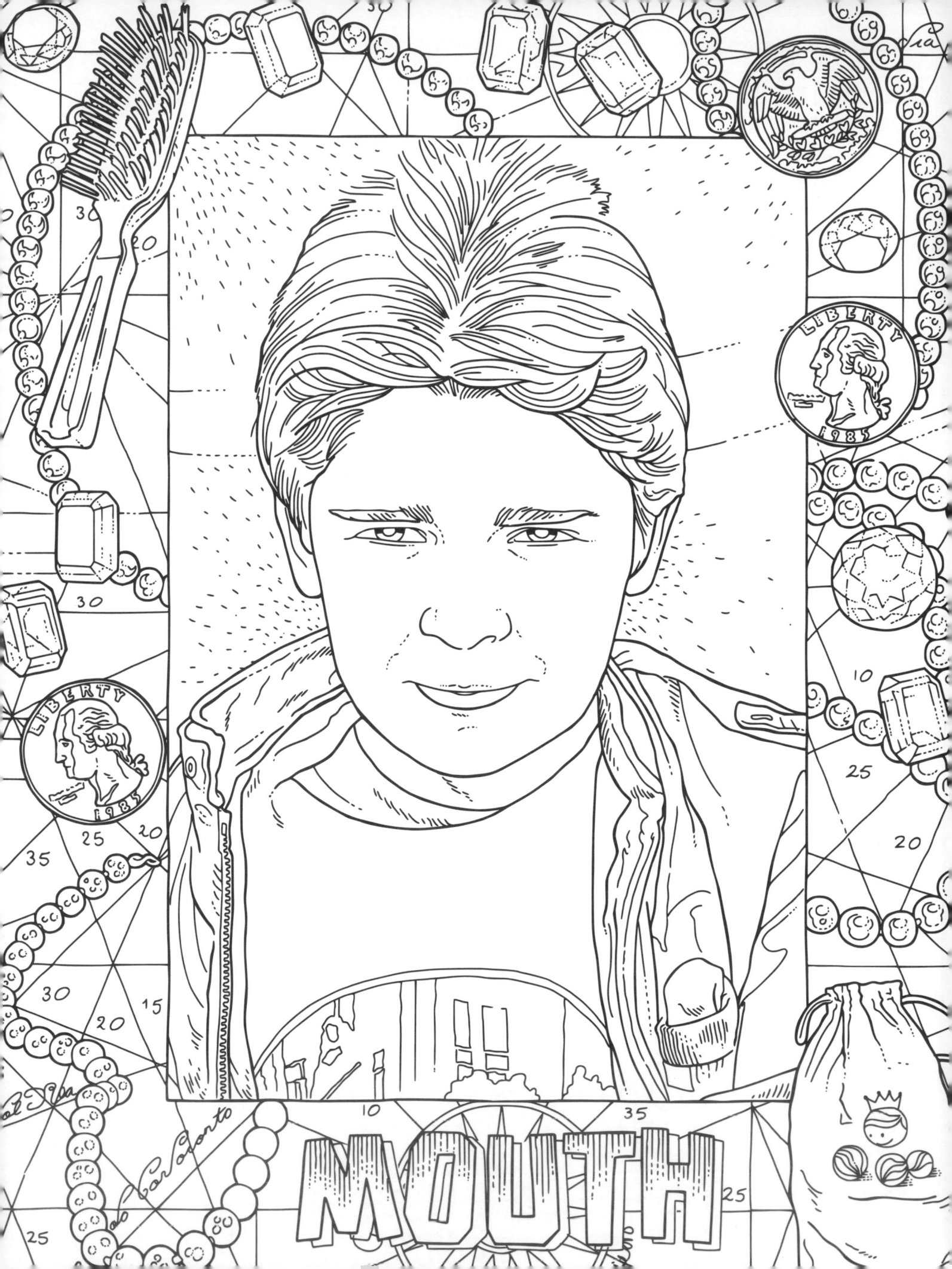
LIBERTY
1985
LIBERTY
1985
MOUTH

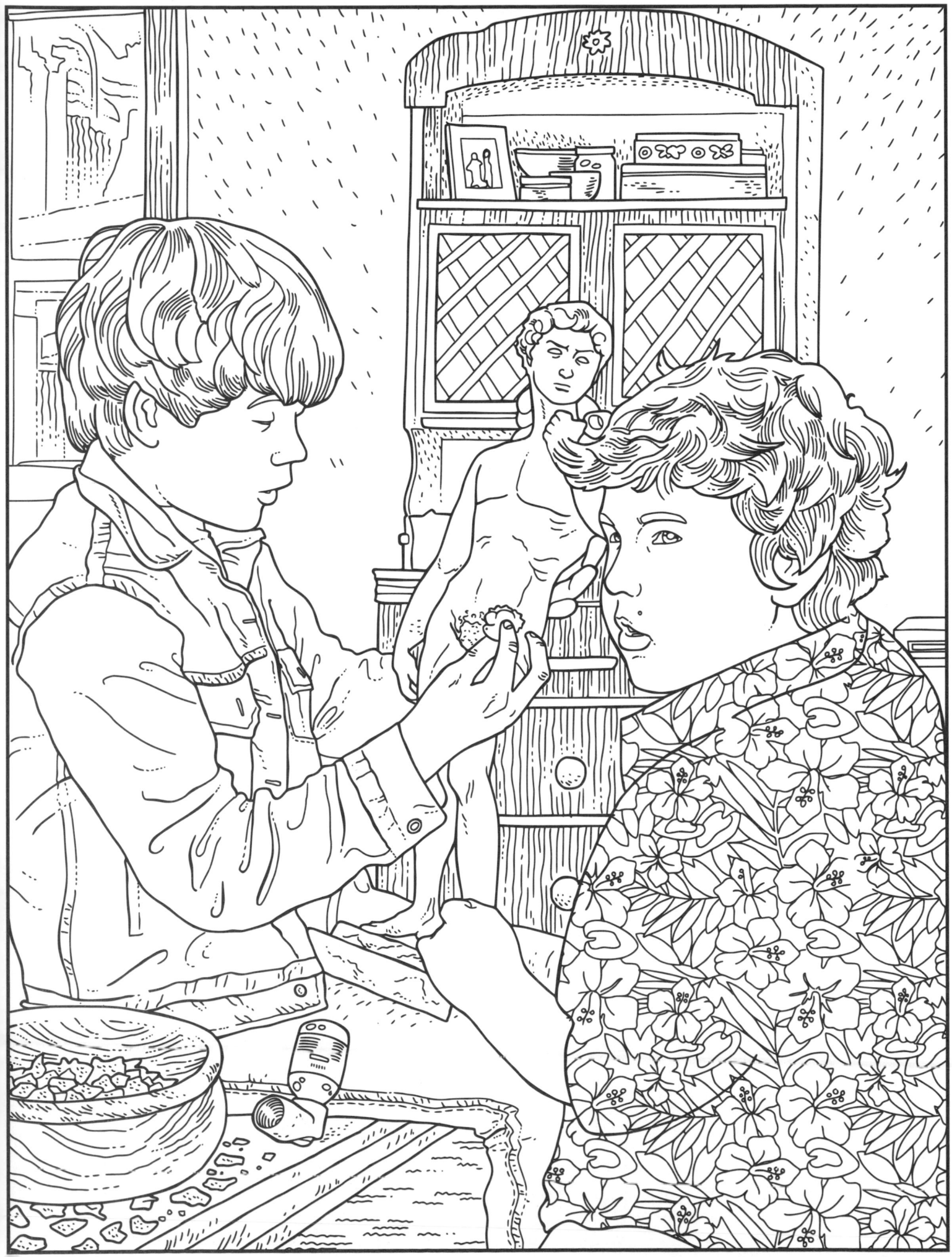

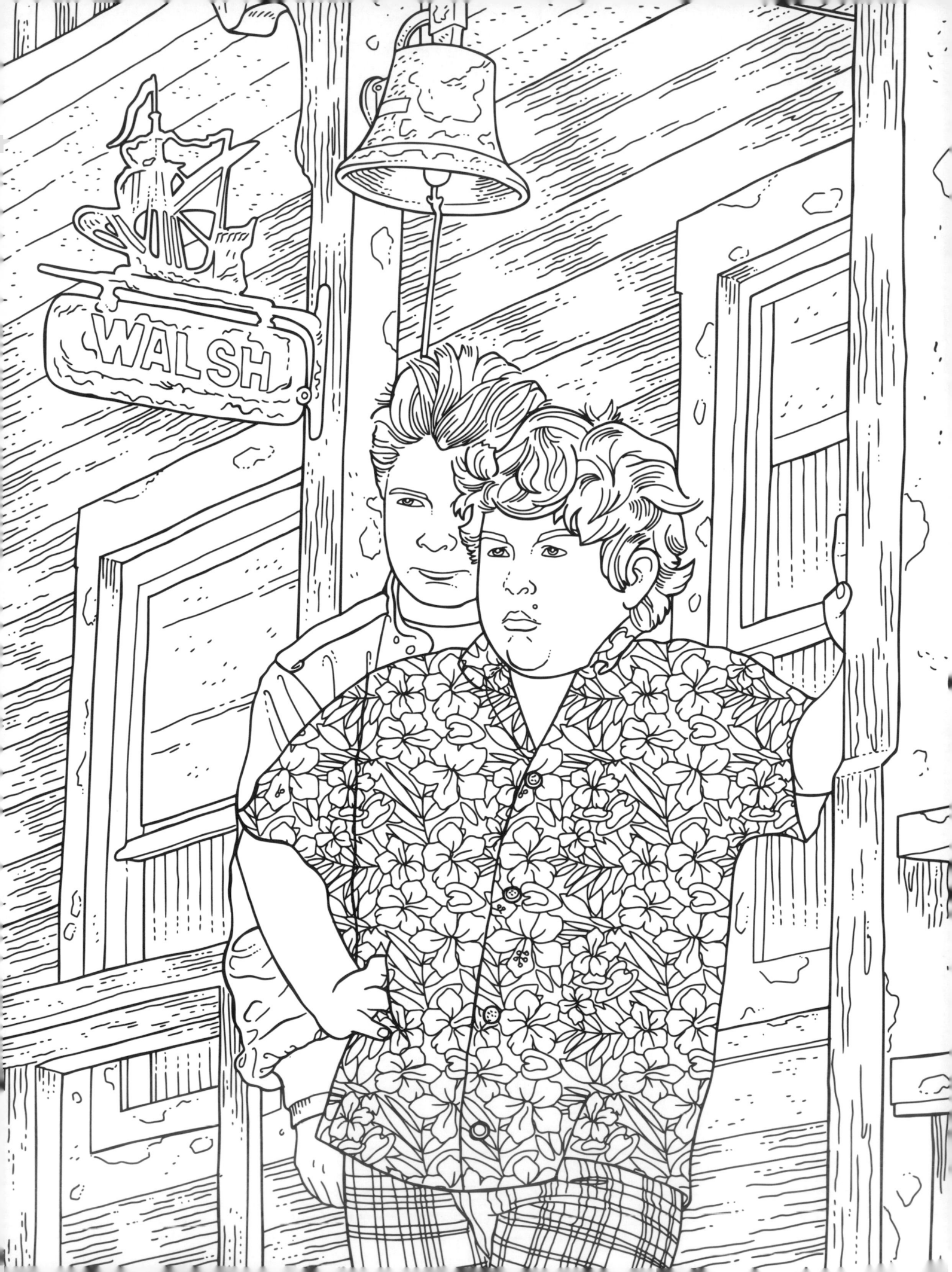
WALSH

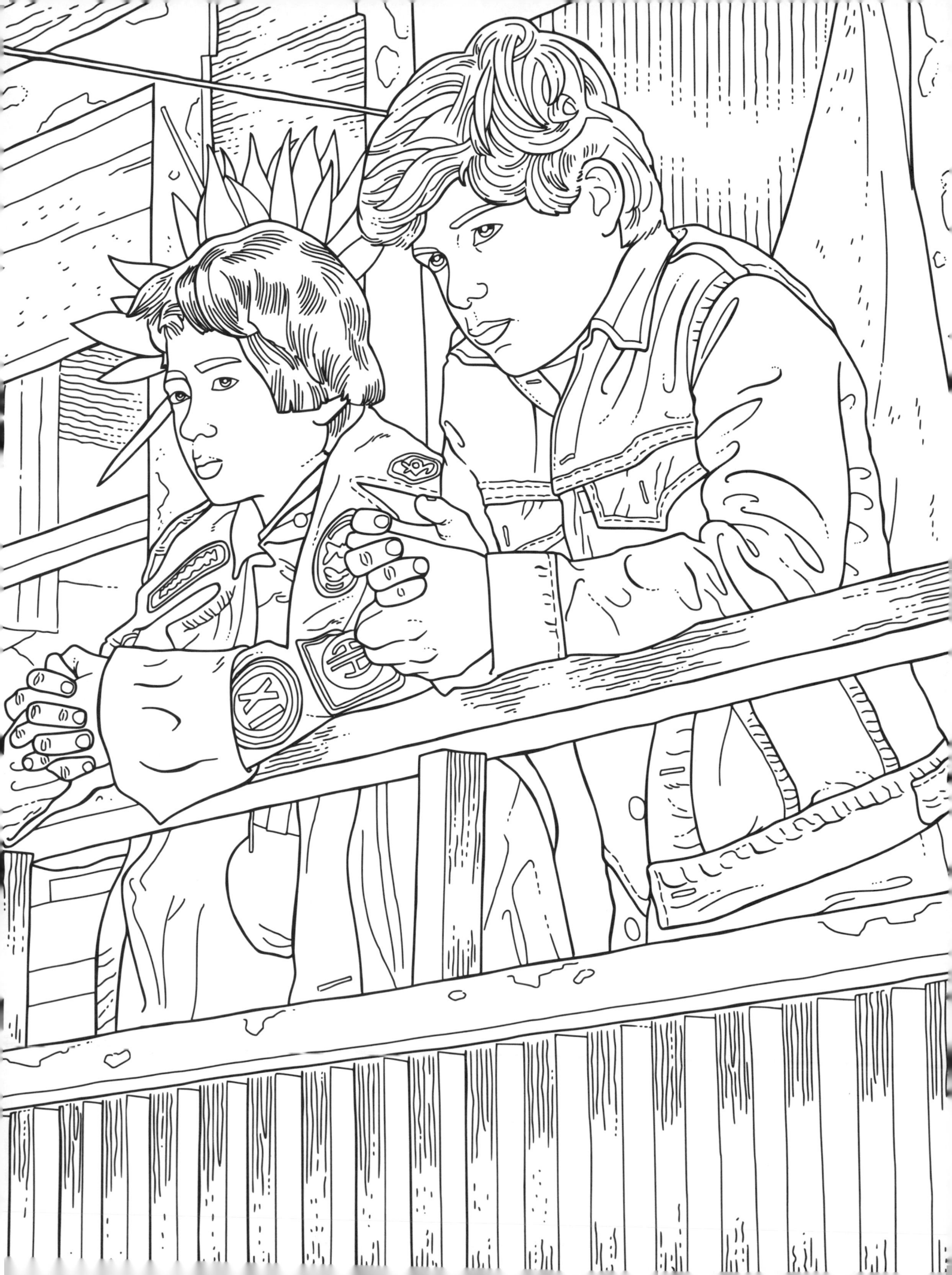

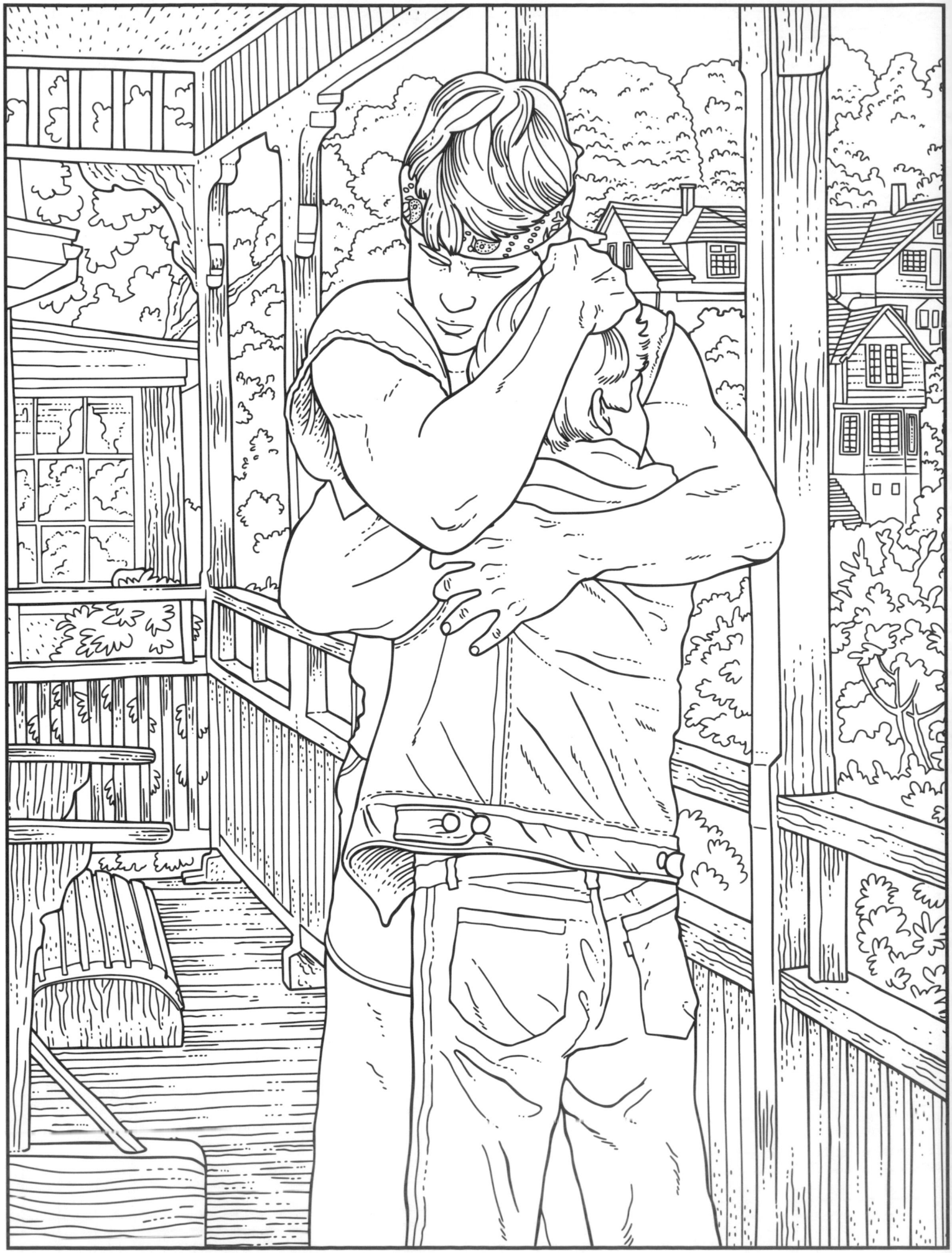

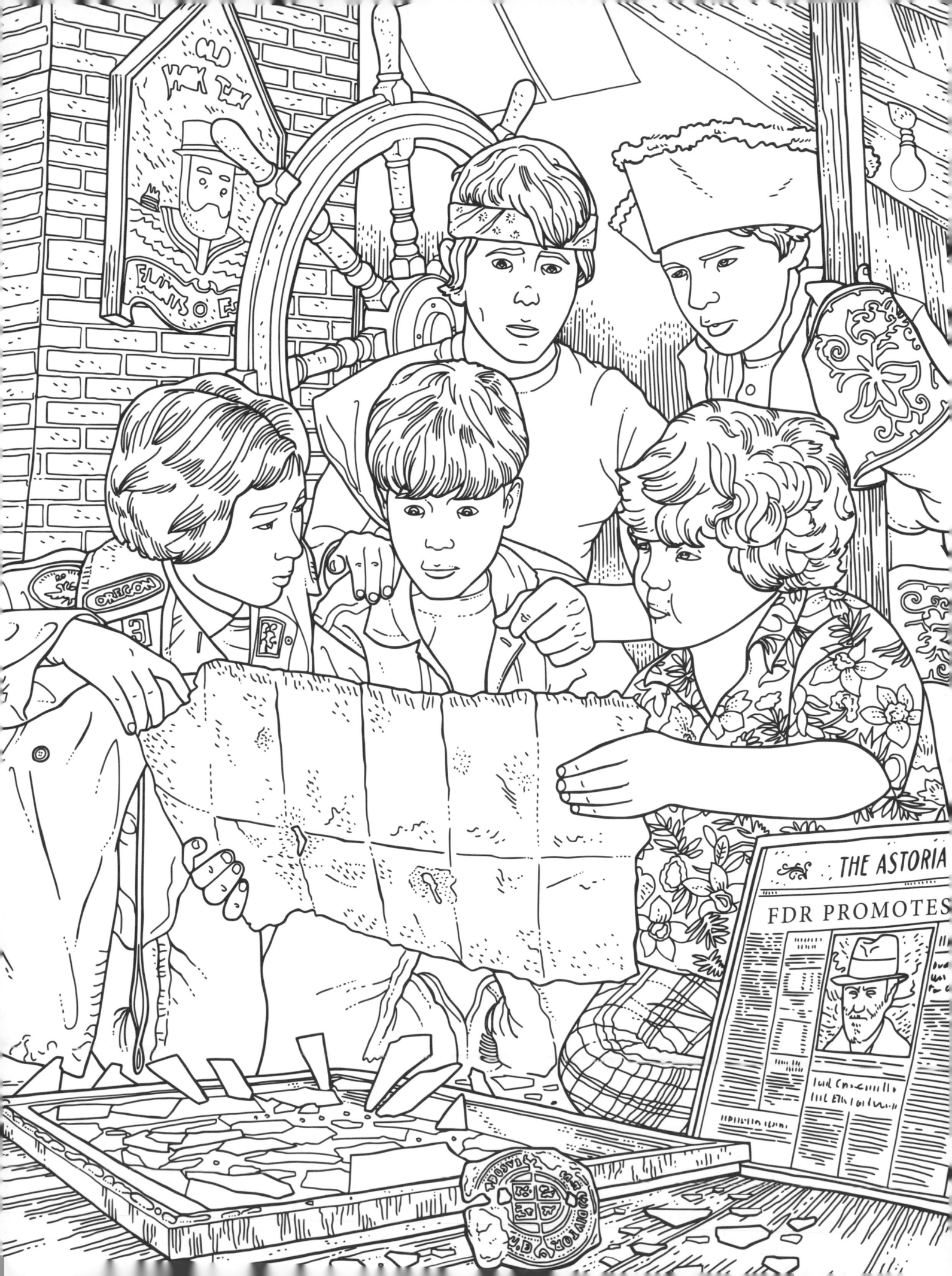
OREGON
THE ASTORIA
FDR PROMOTES

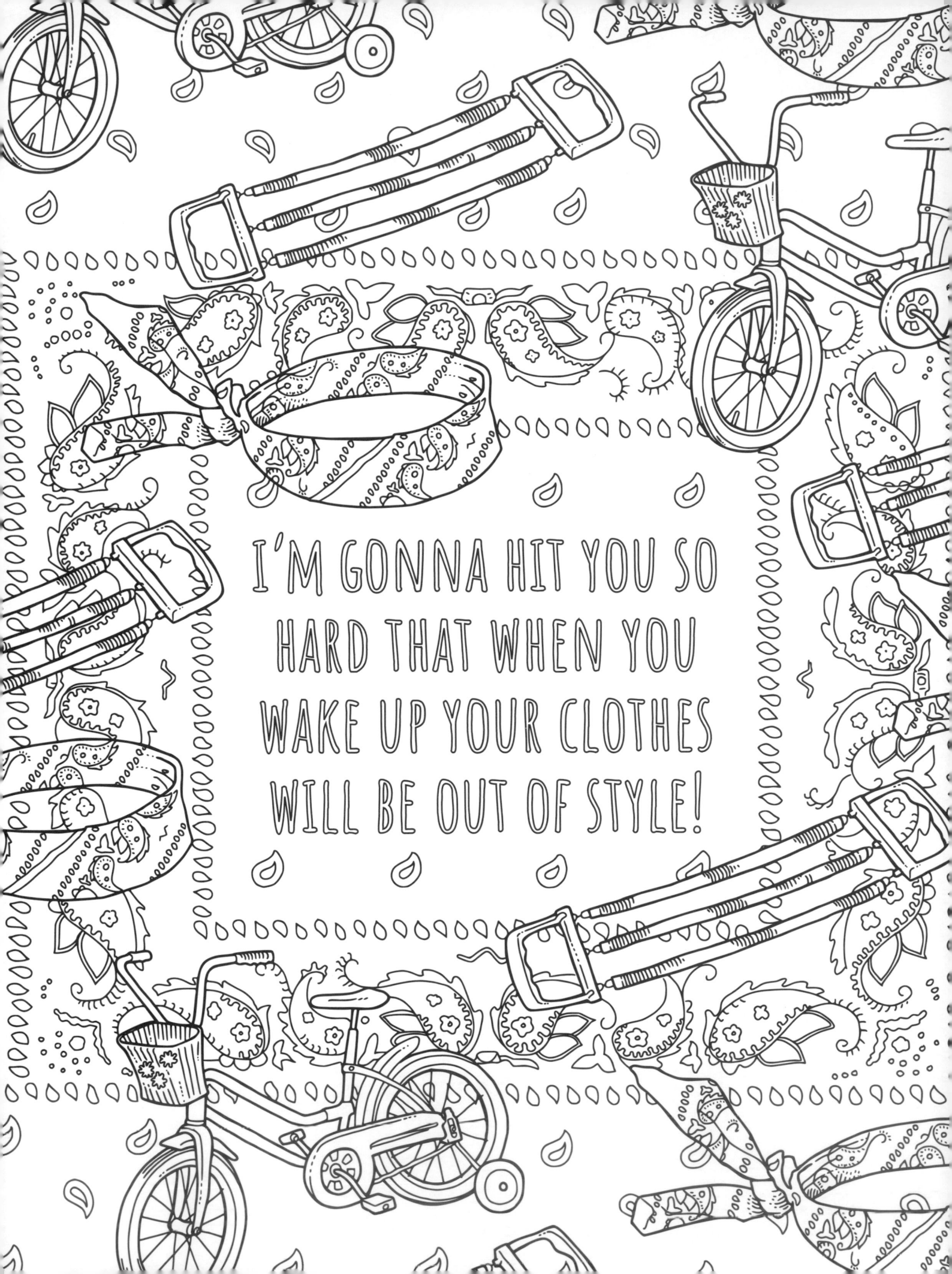
I'M GONNA HIT YOU SO
HARD THAT WHEN YOU
WAKE UP YOUR CLOTHES
WILL BE OUT OF STYLE!

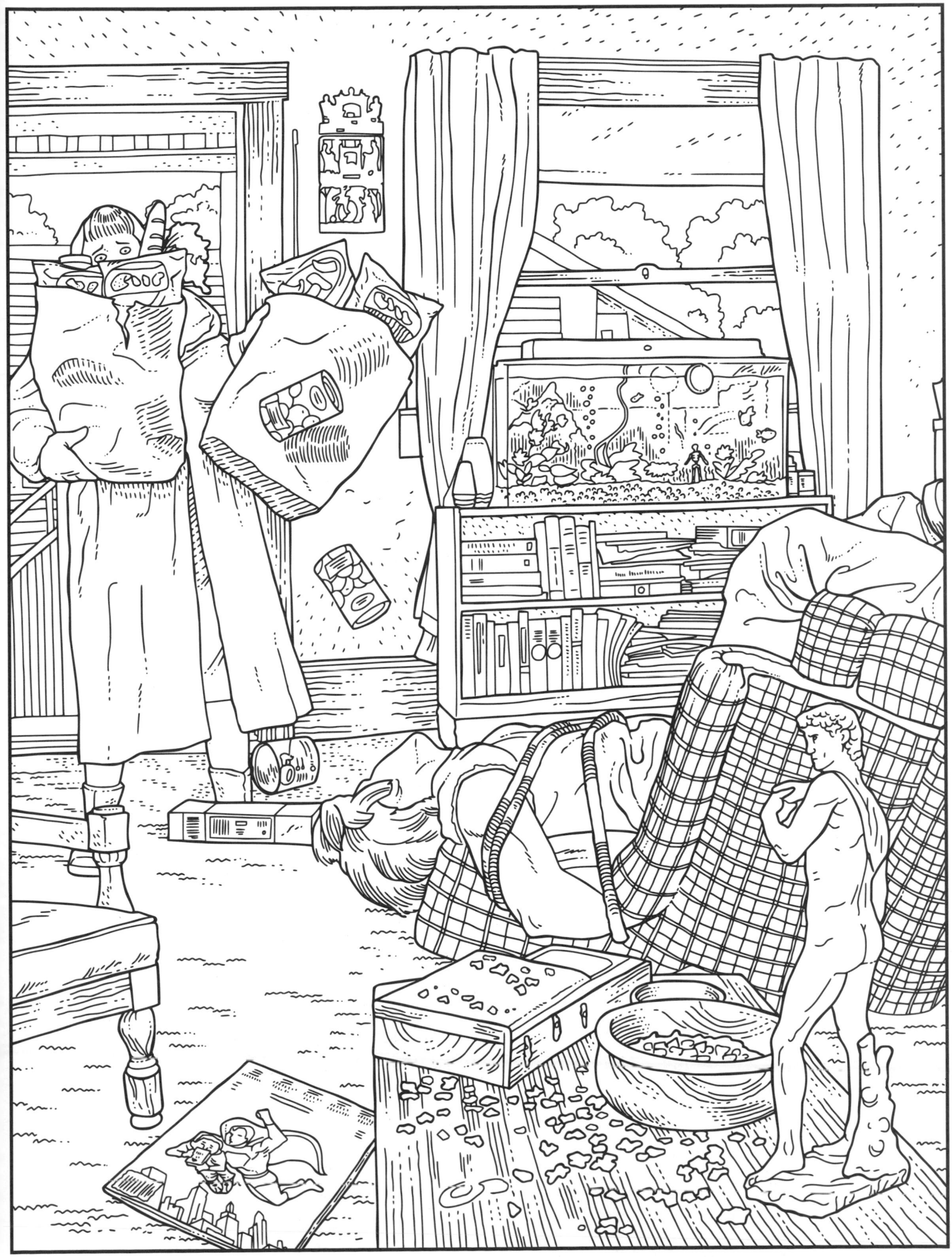

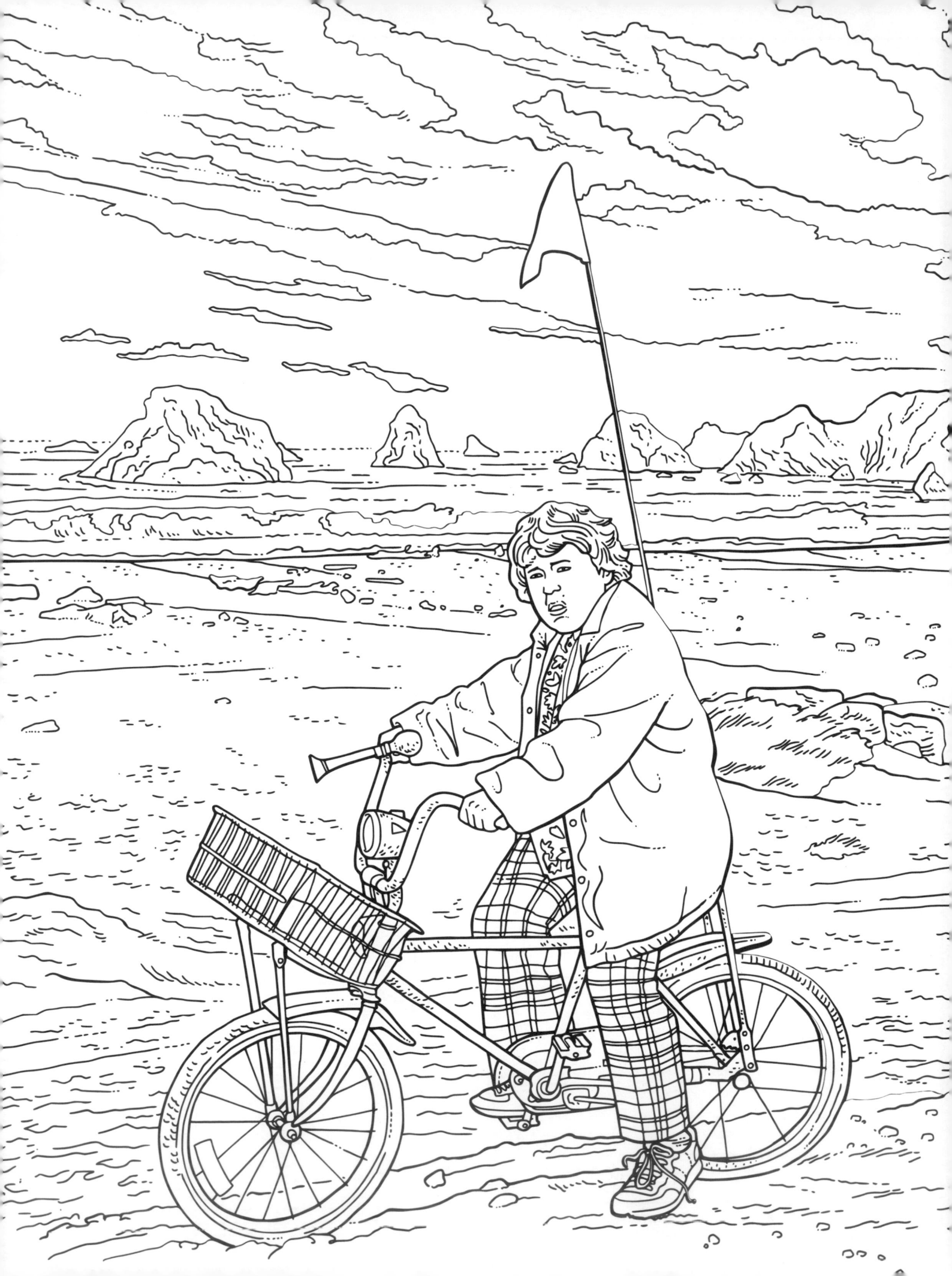

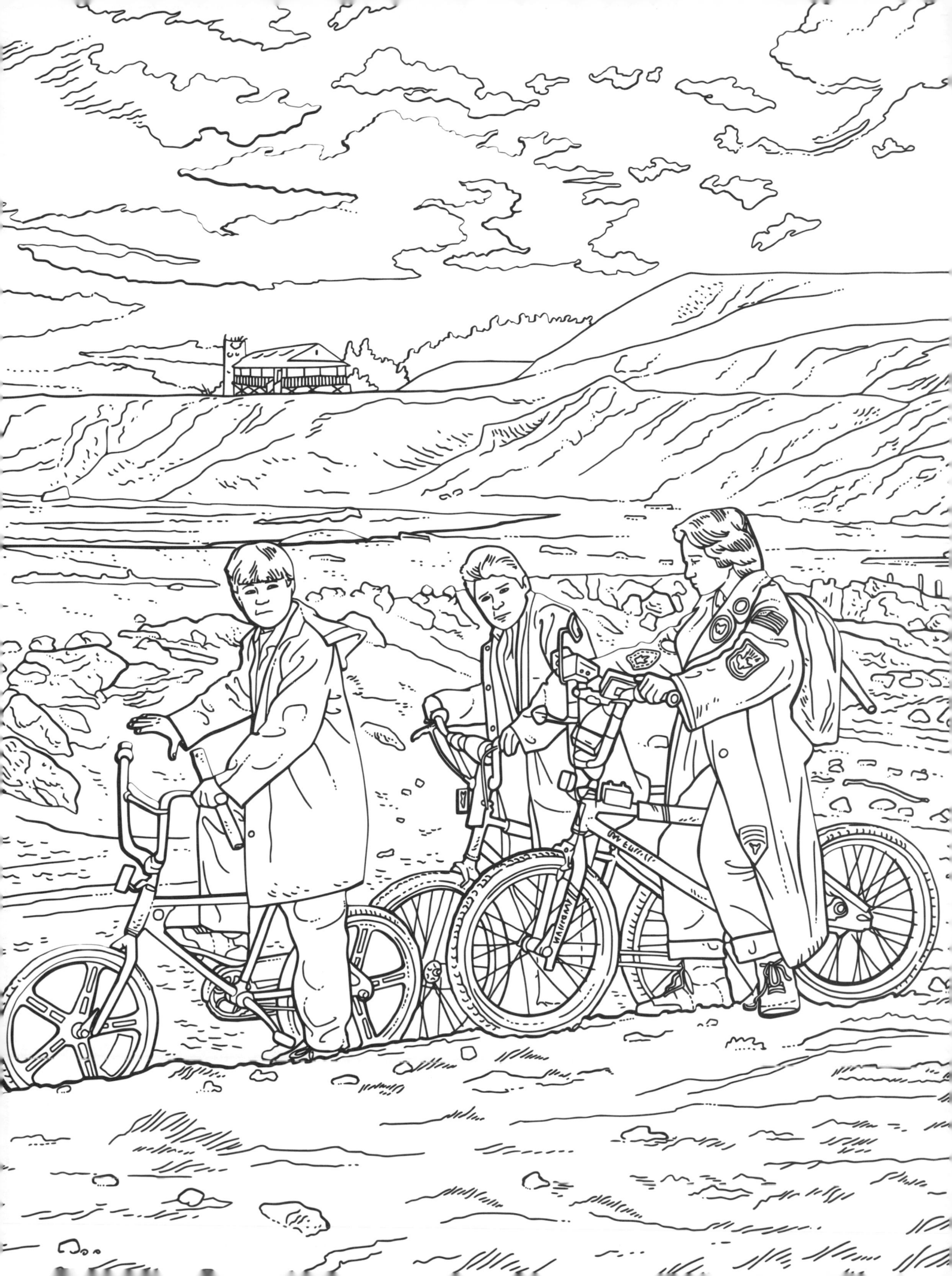

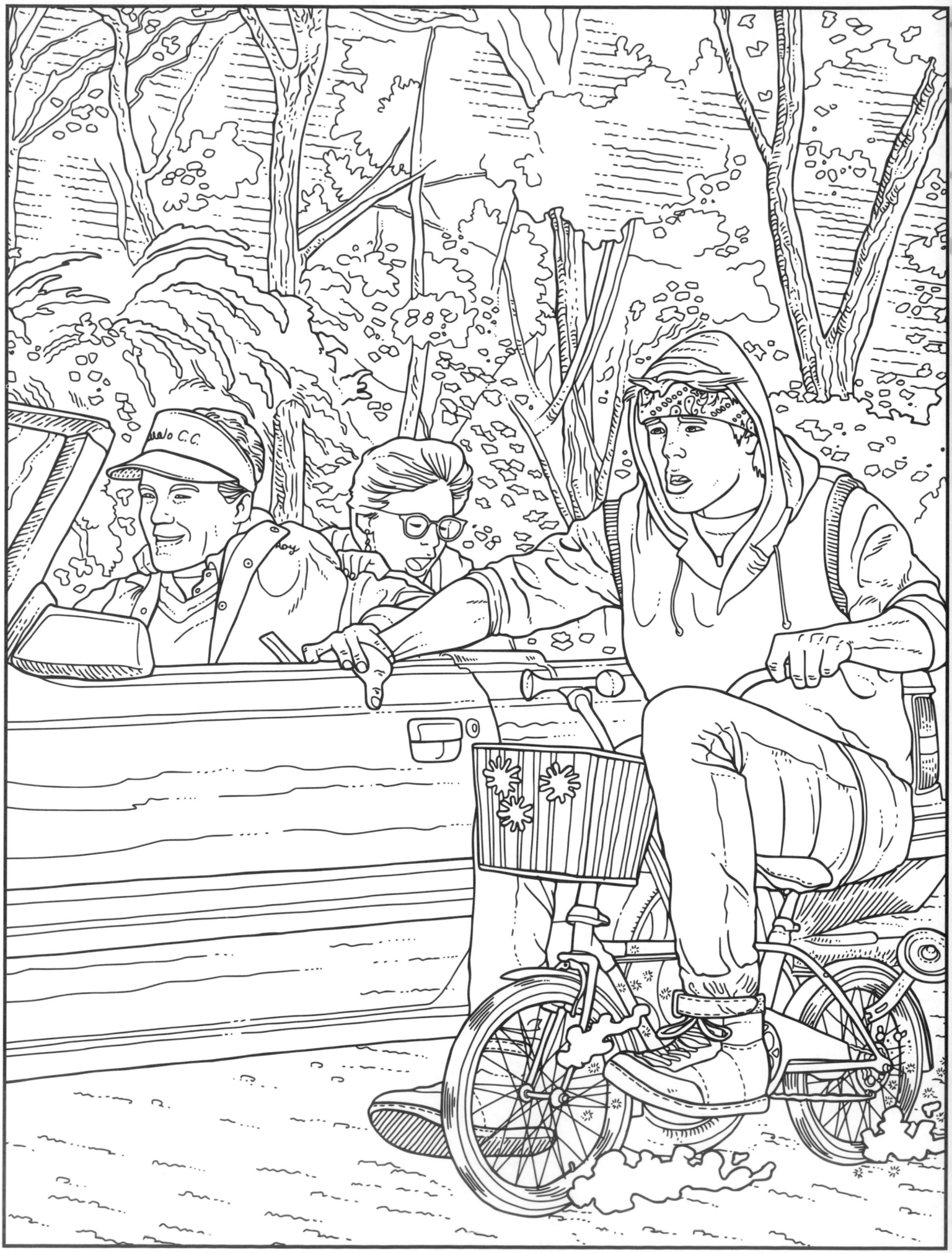

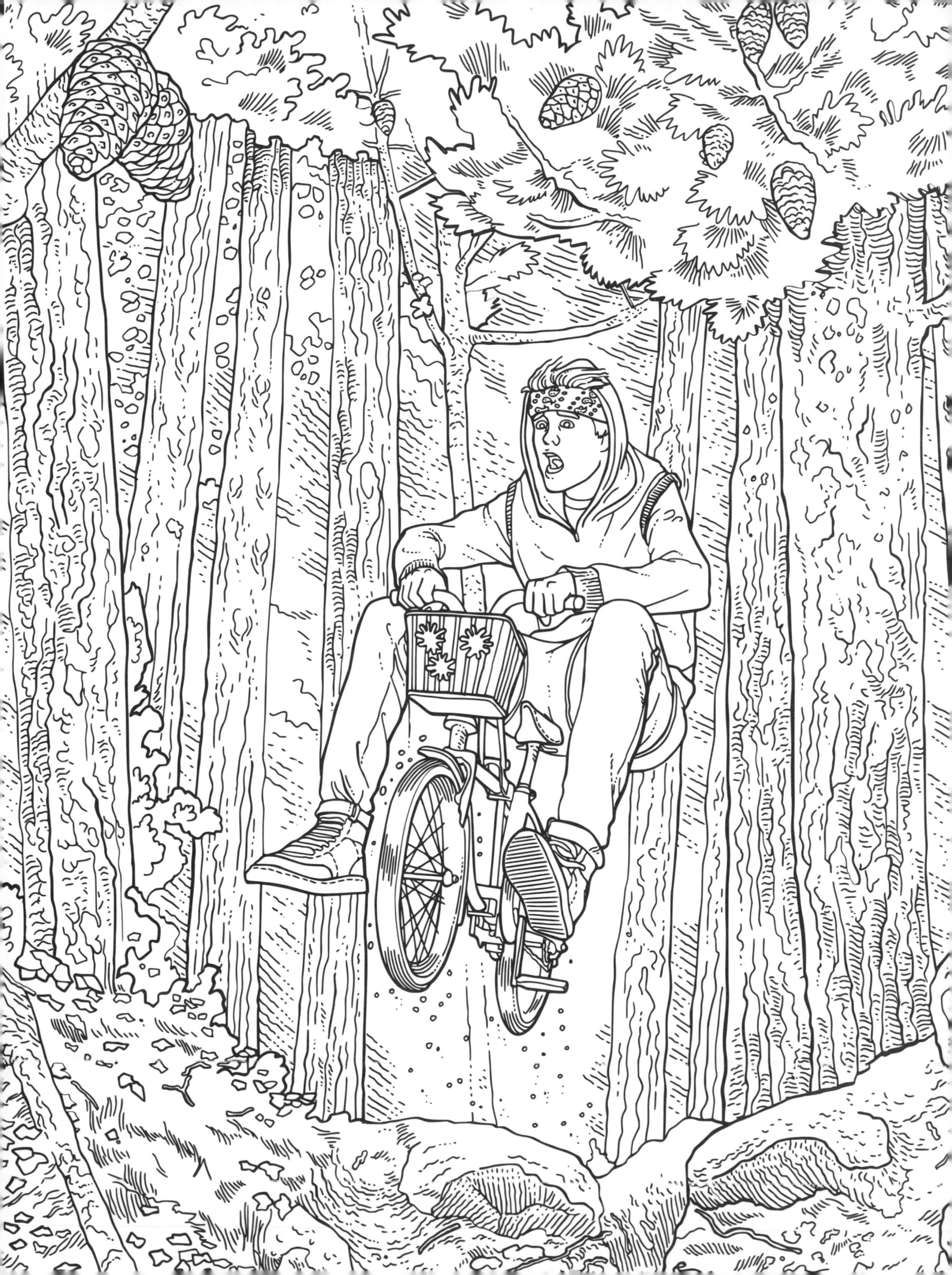

OSVI
ANTOLAN

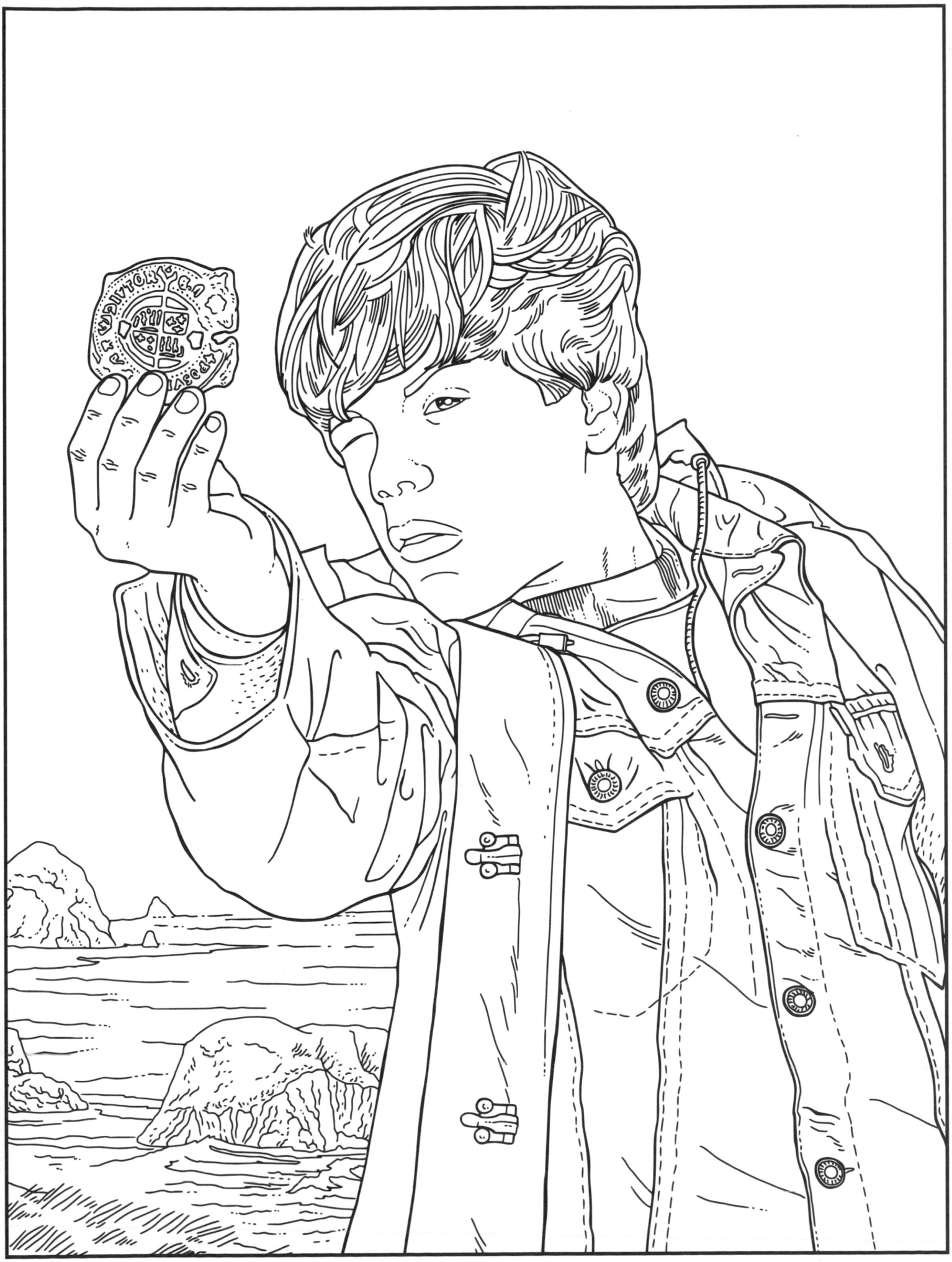

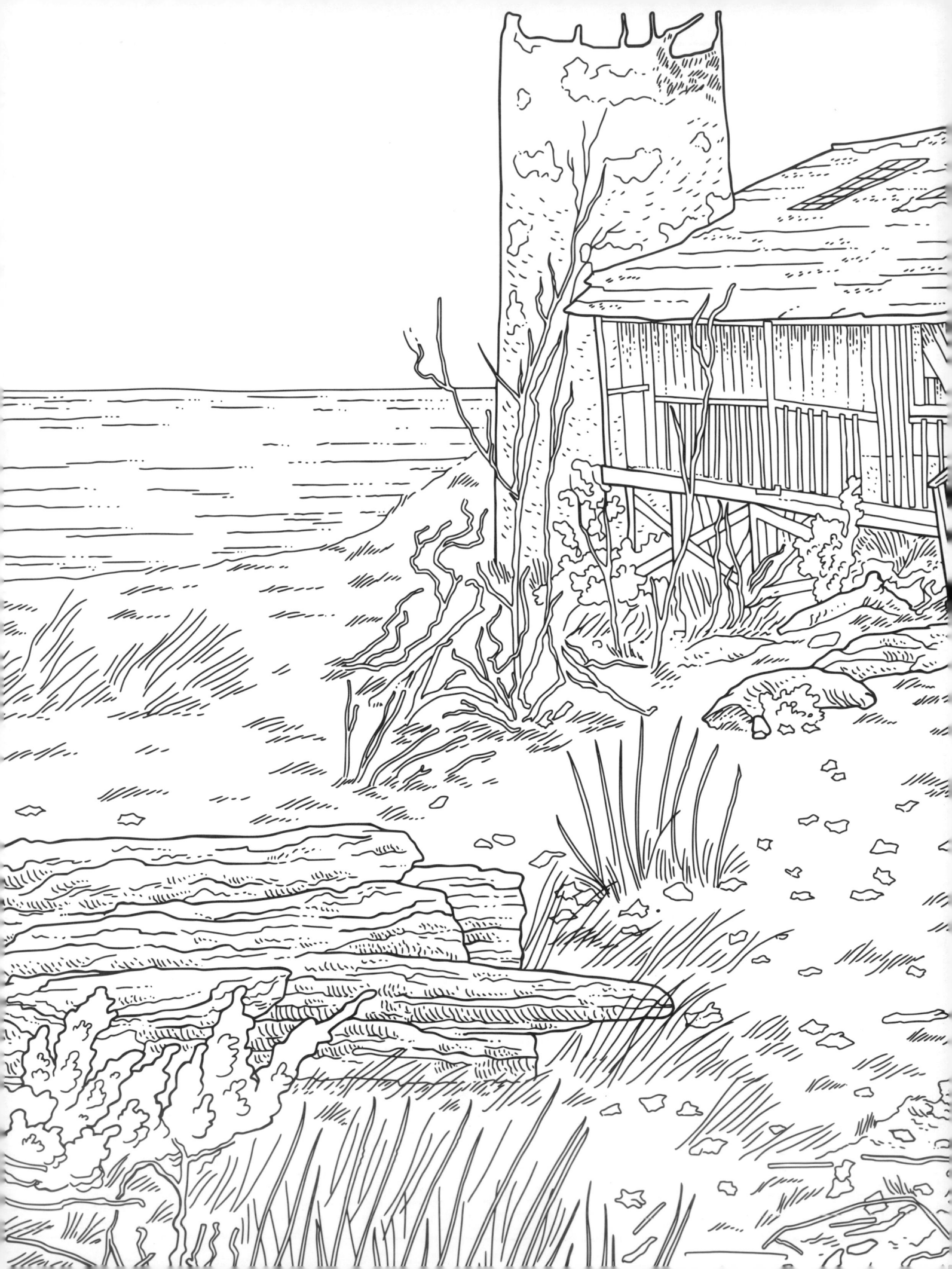

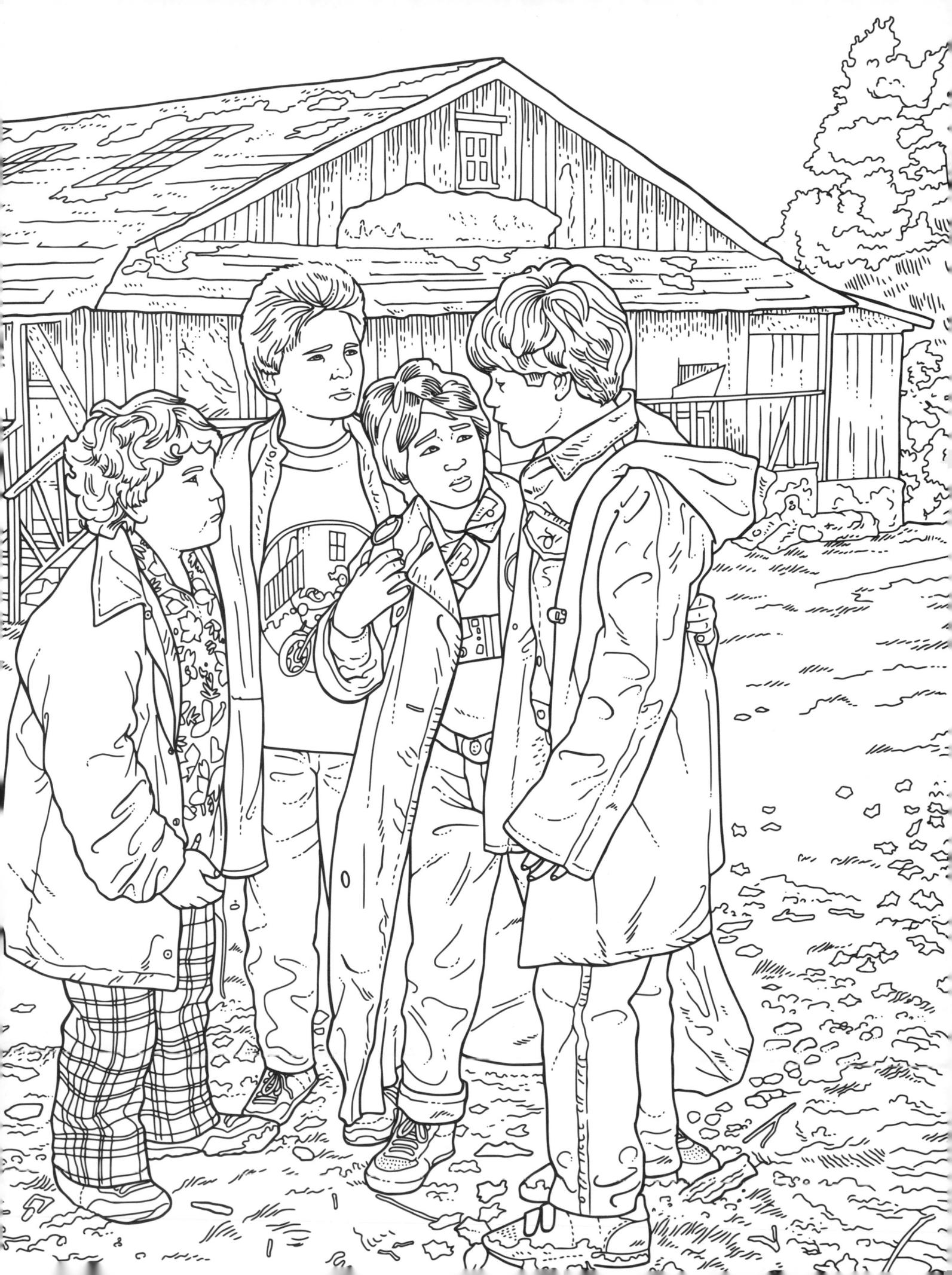

WANTED
A11058E
A91068
A81300

962

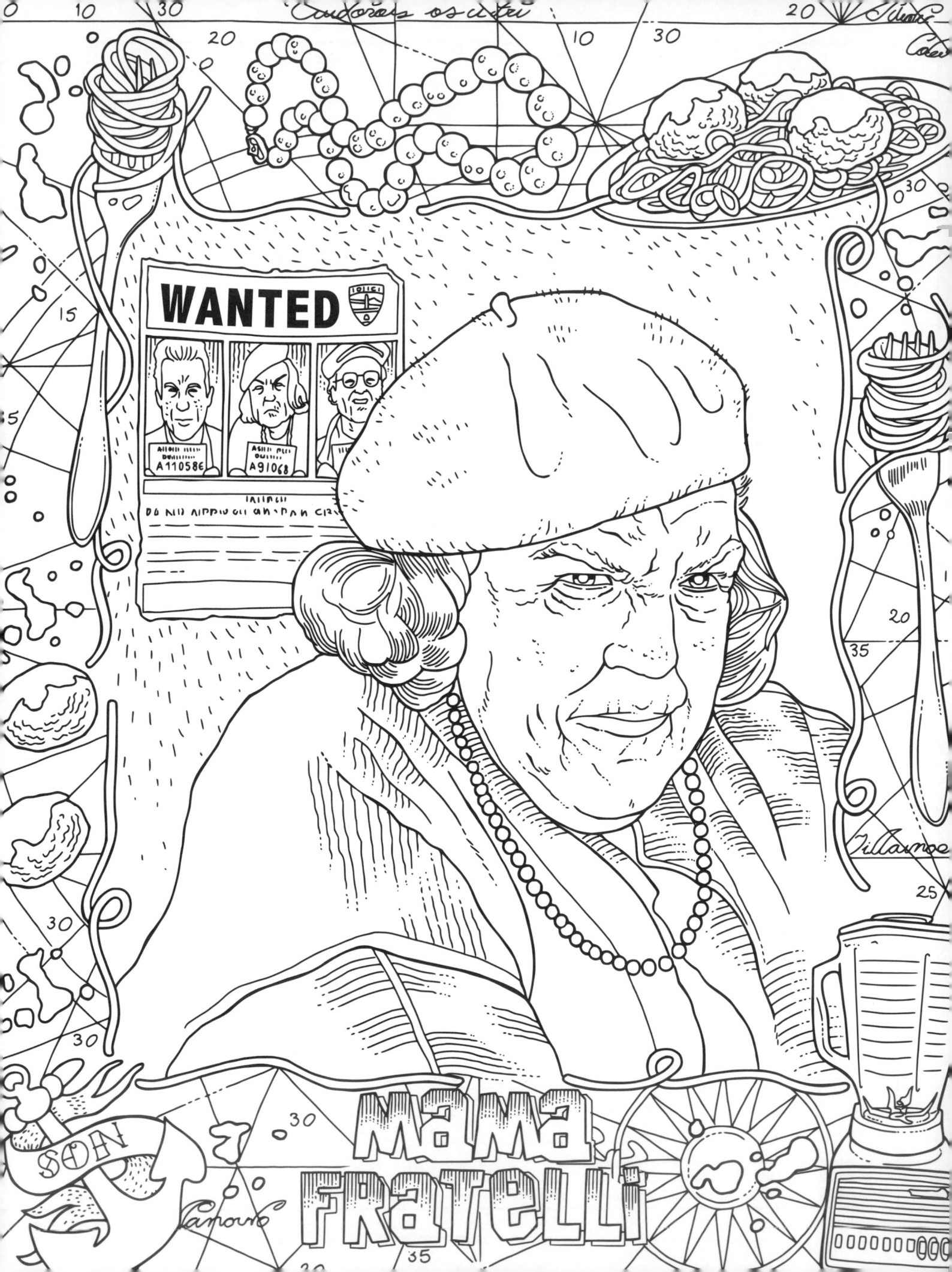
WANTED
A11058€
A91068
Mama
Fratelli
SON

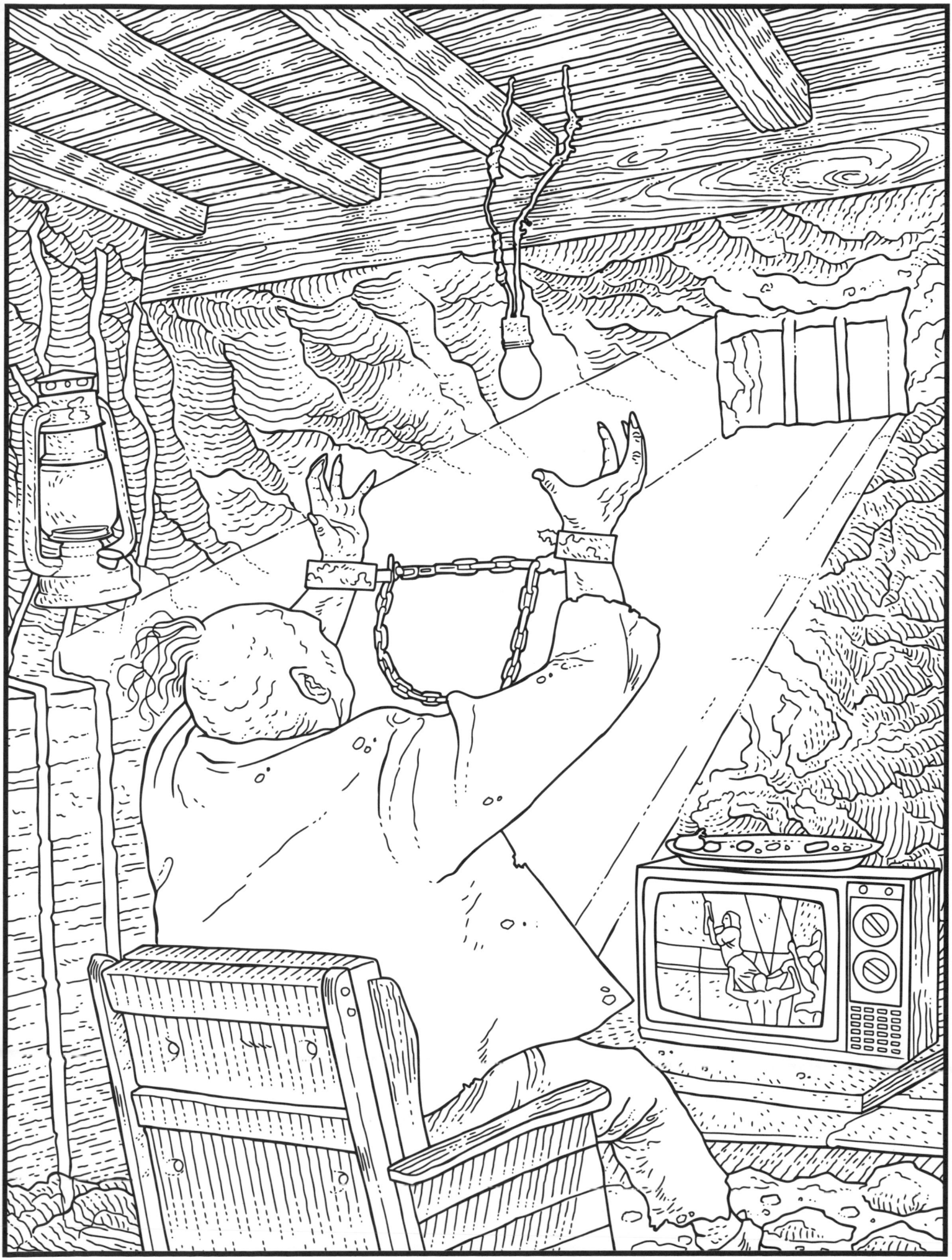

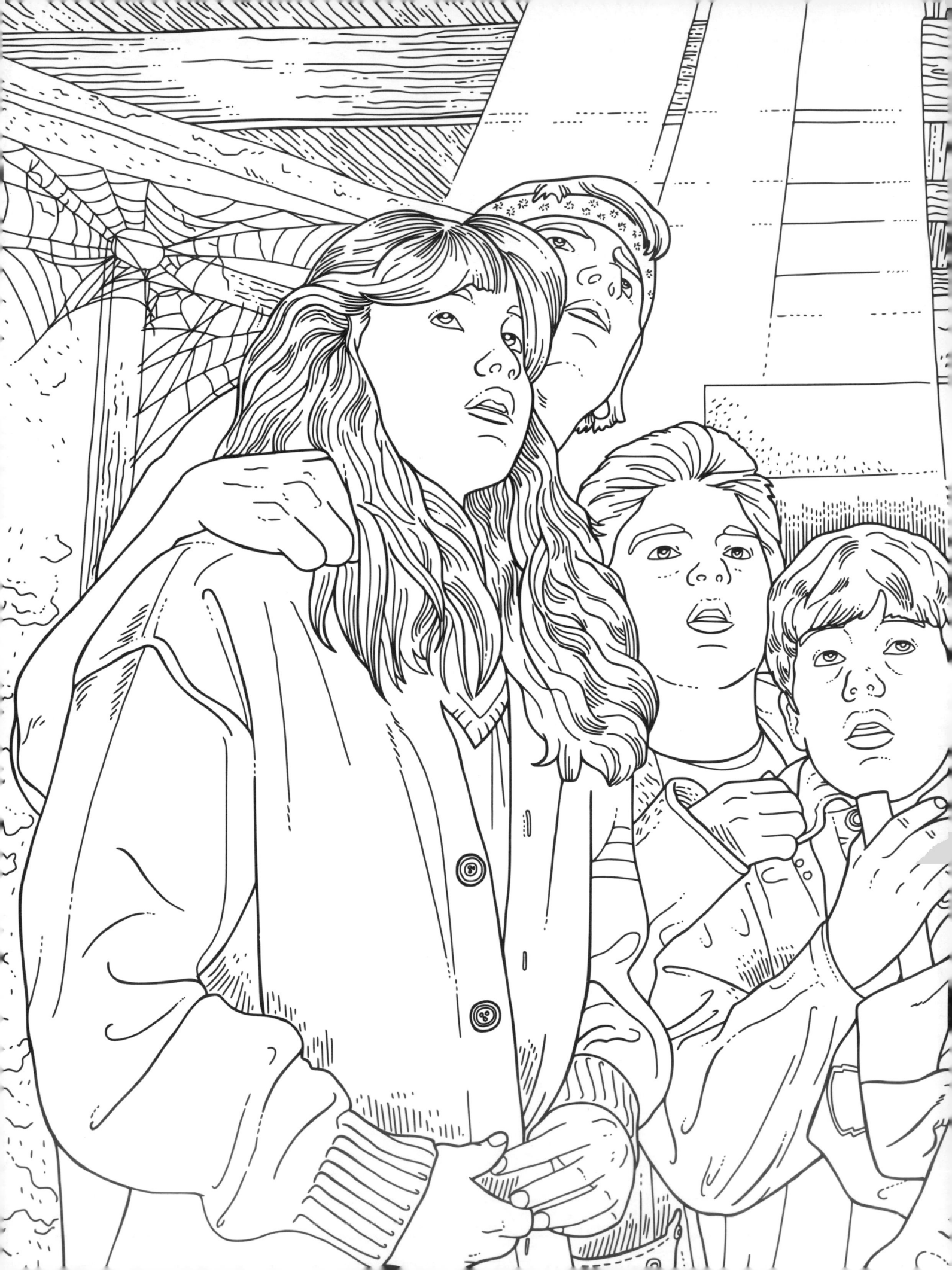

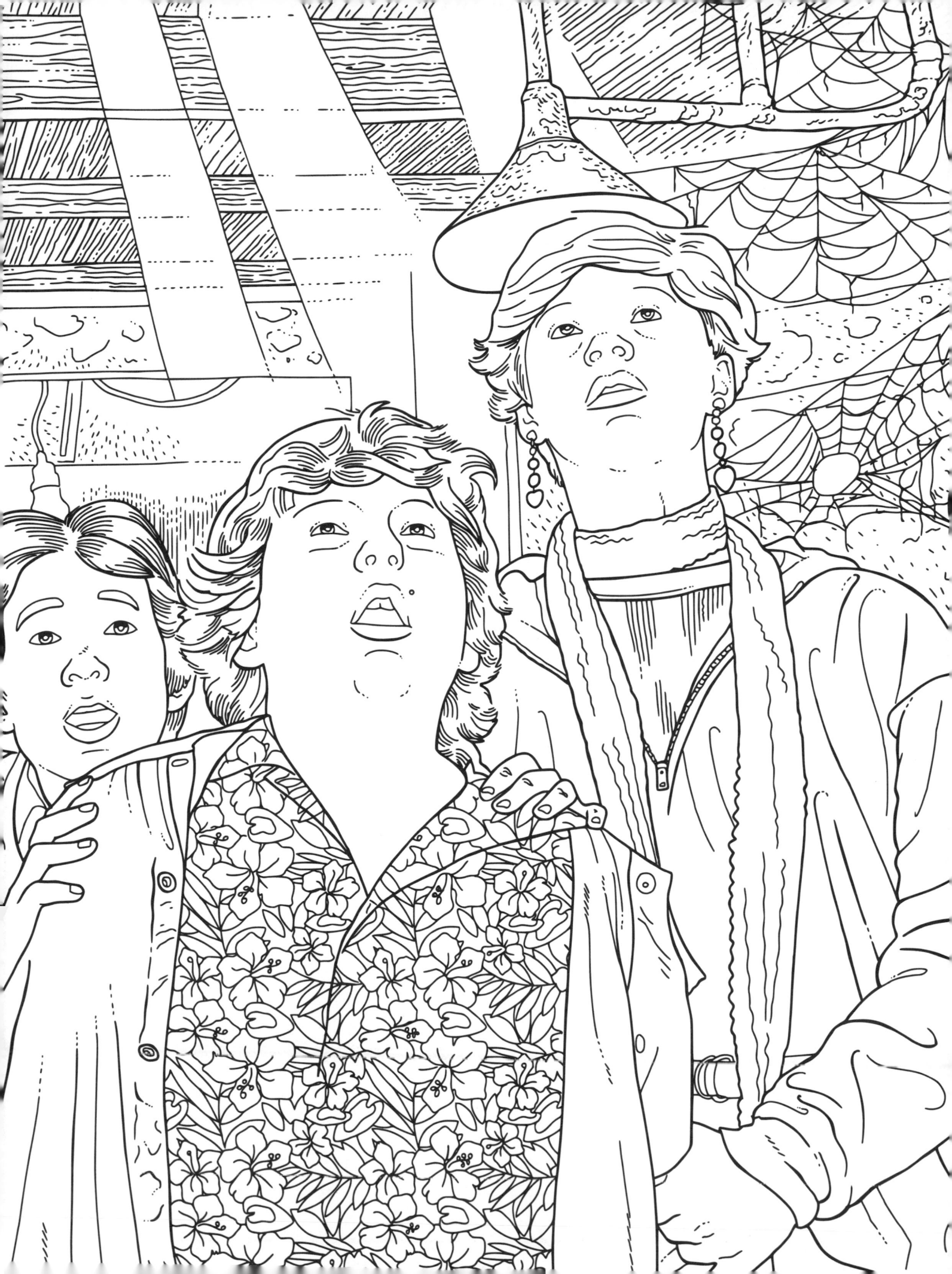

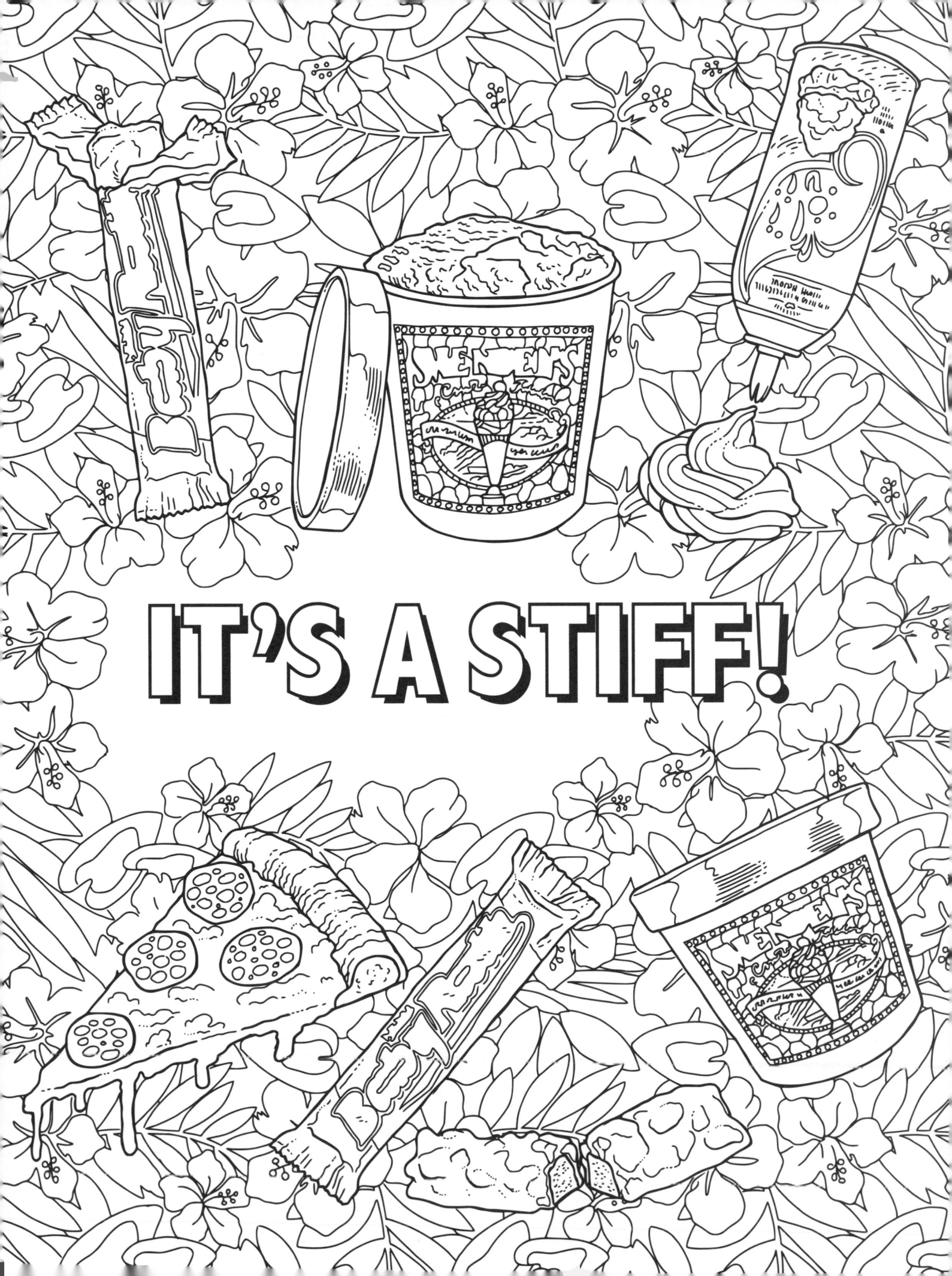
IT'S A STIFF!

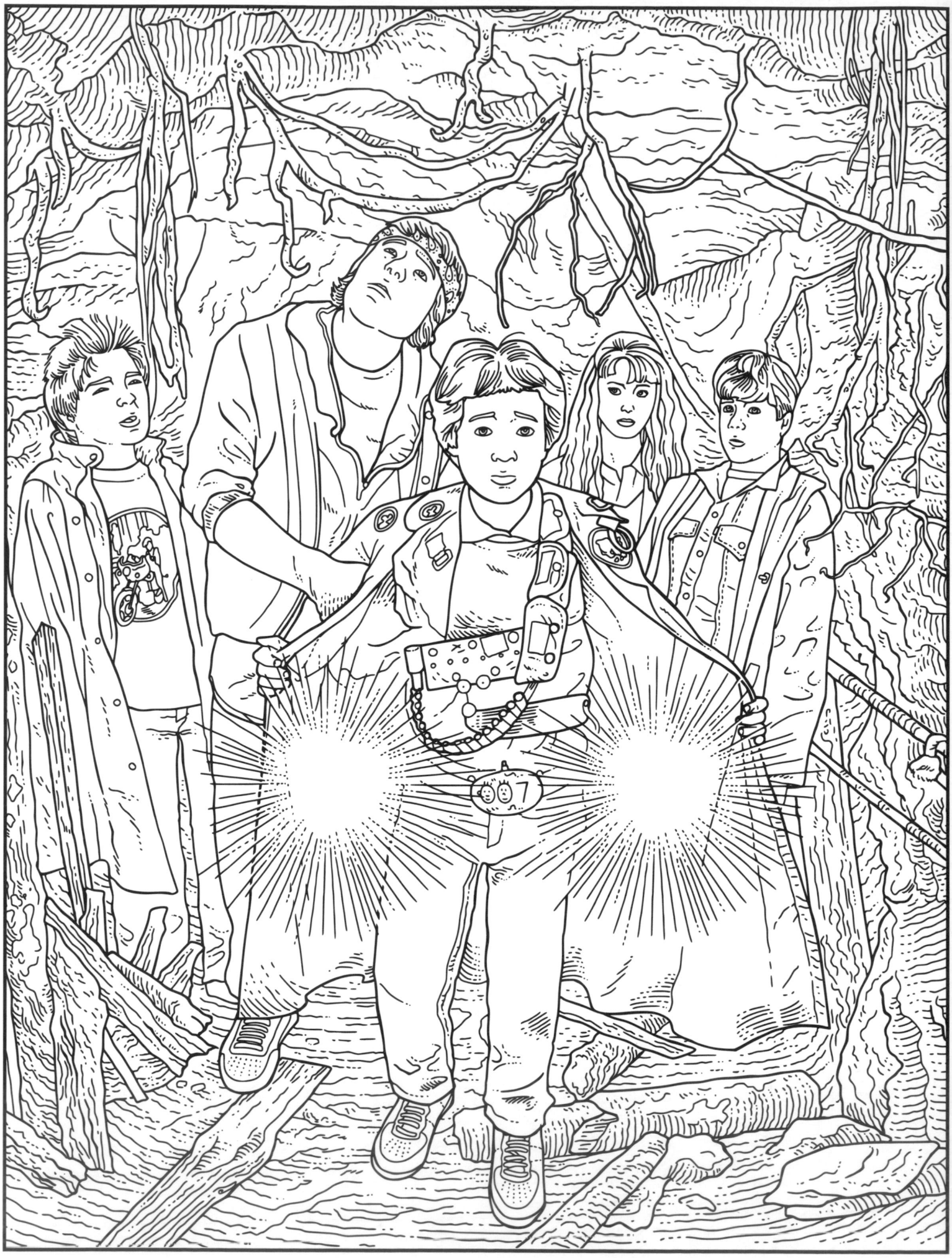

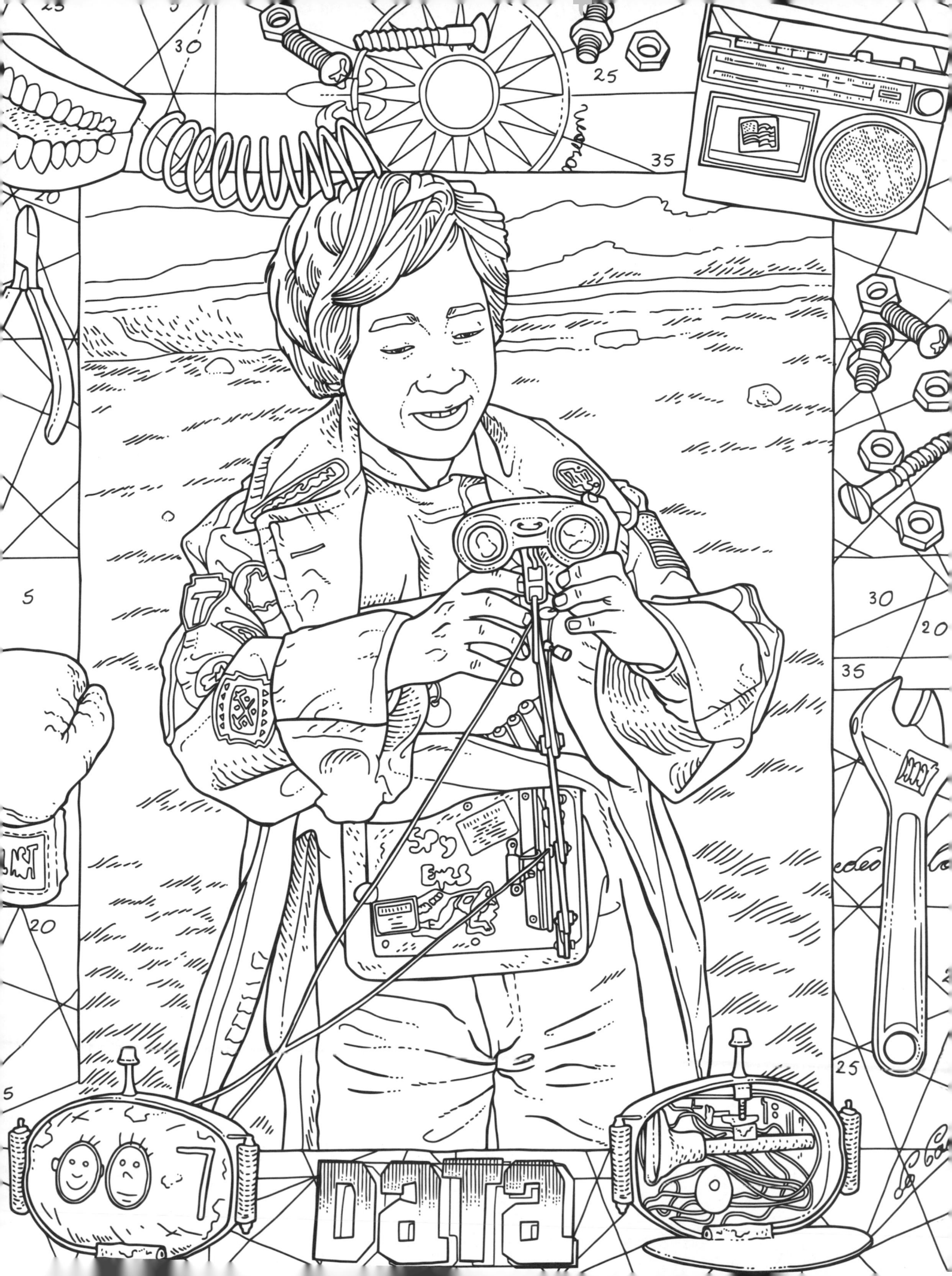
data

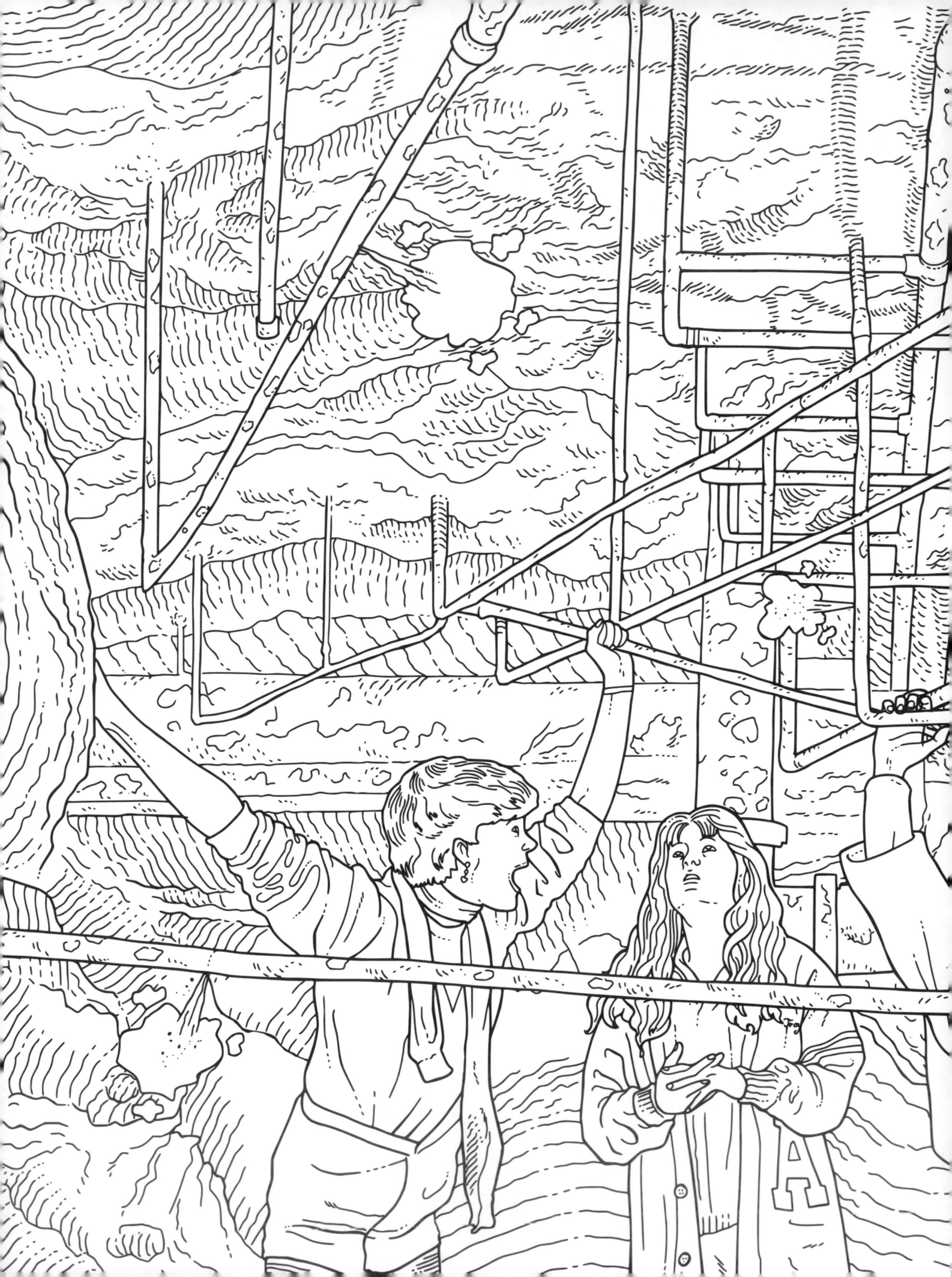
A

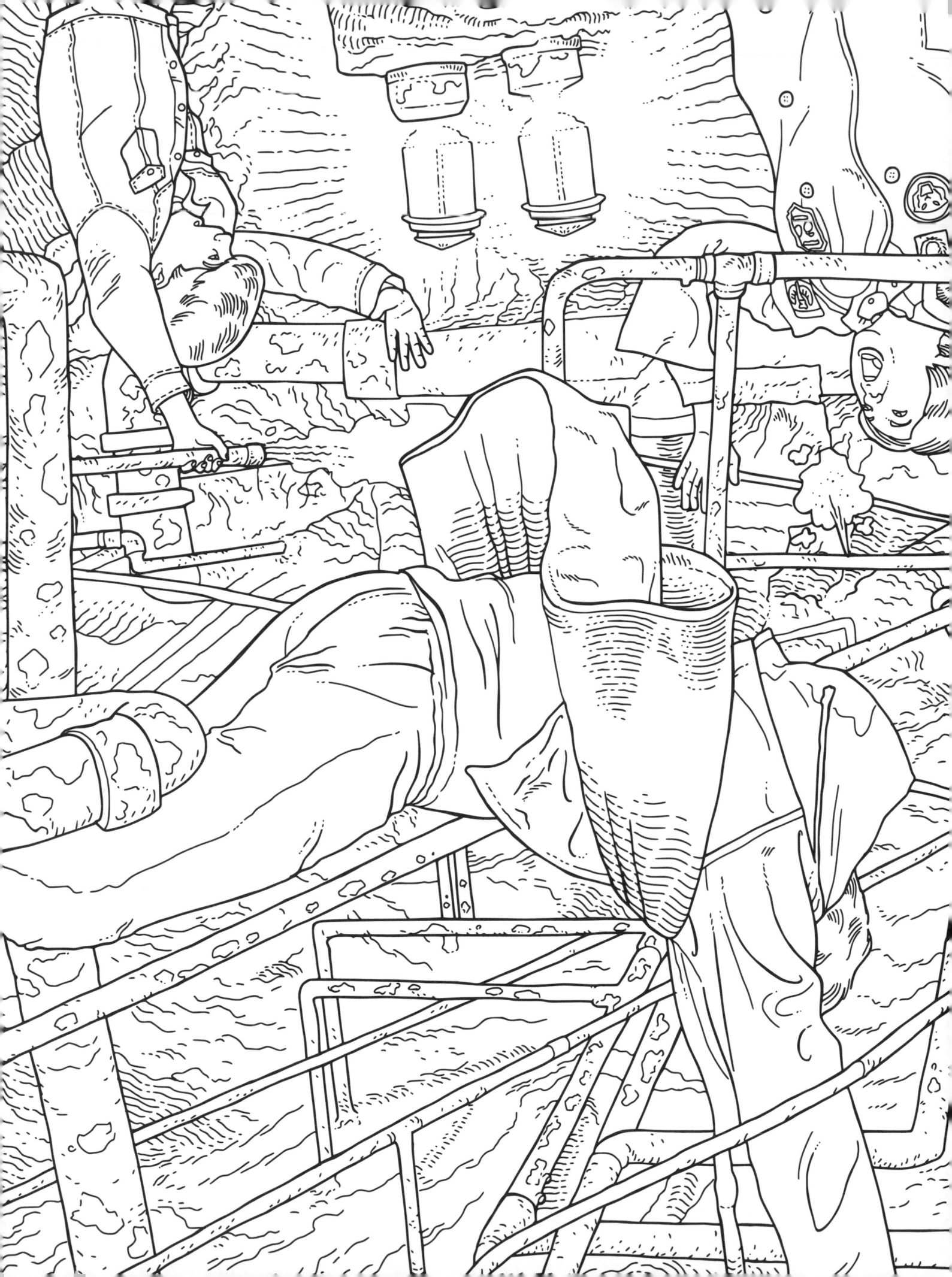

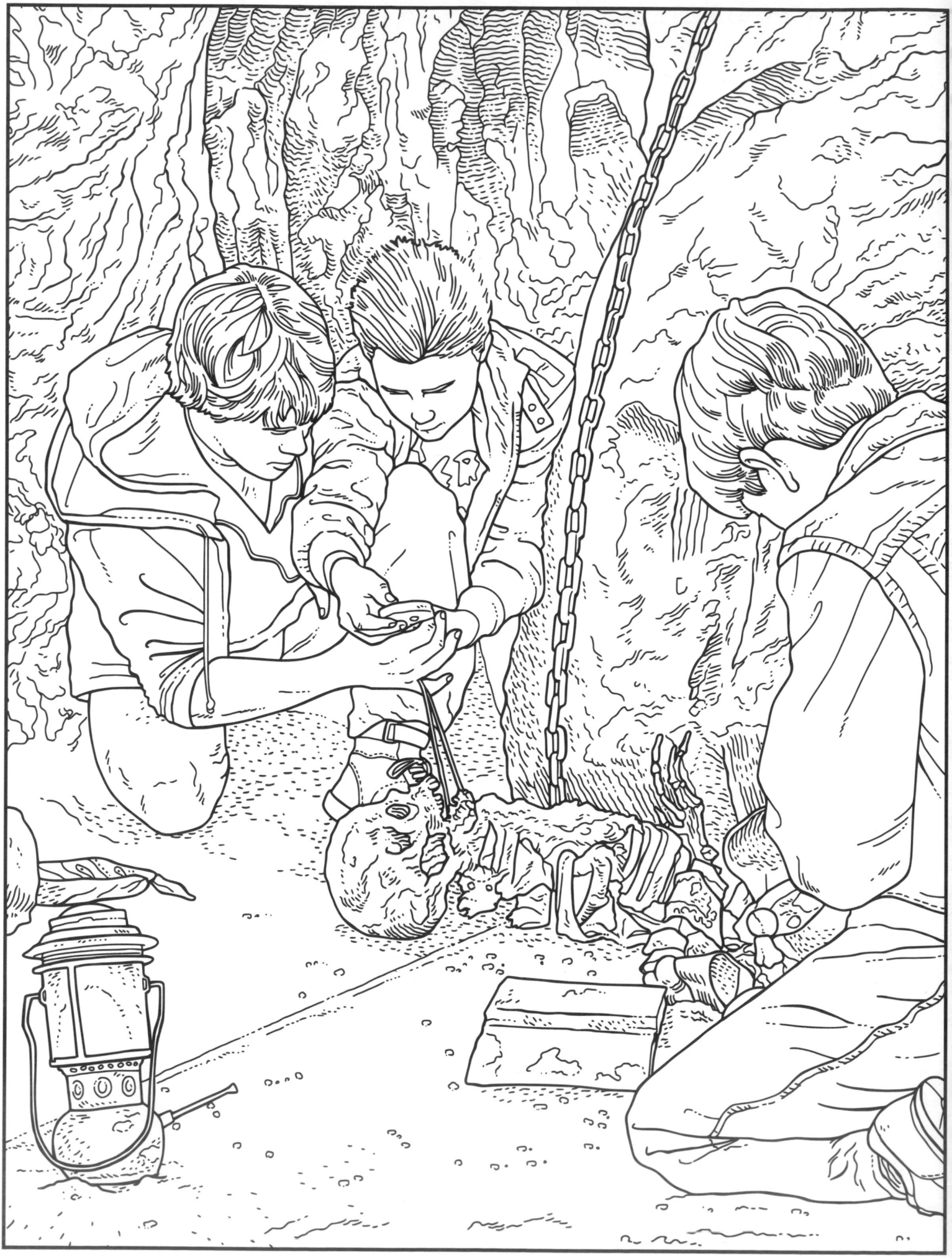

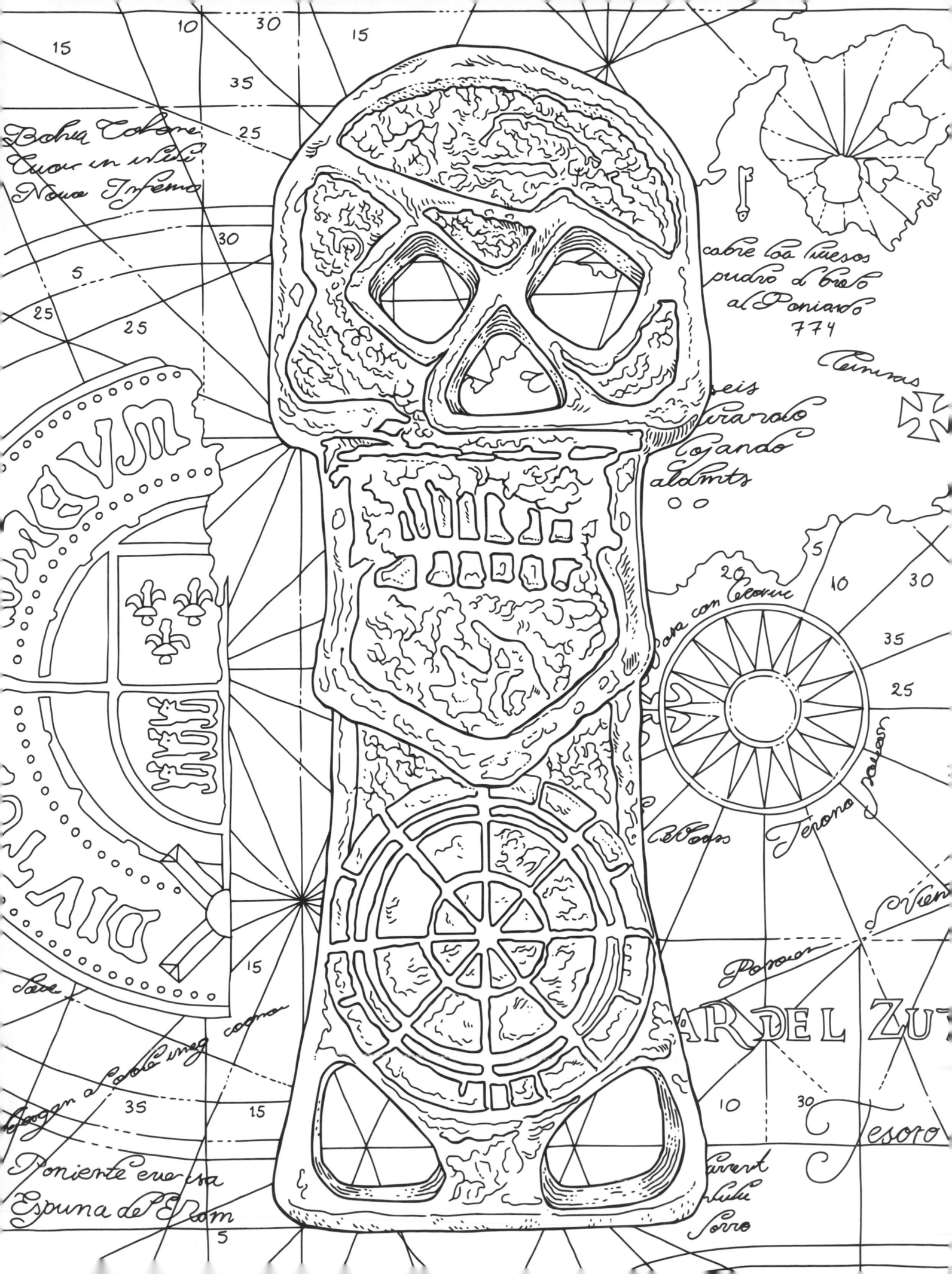
Bahia Colone
Cuor in vitti
Nova Inferno
cabre los huesos
pudro el brazo
al Poniardo
774
Cumbras
Jerona
Tesoro
Poniente eve sa
Espuna de Elom

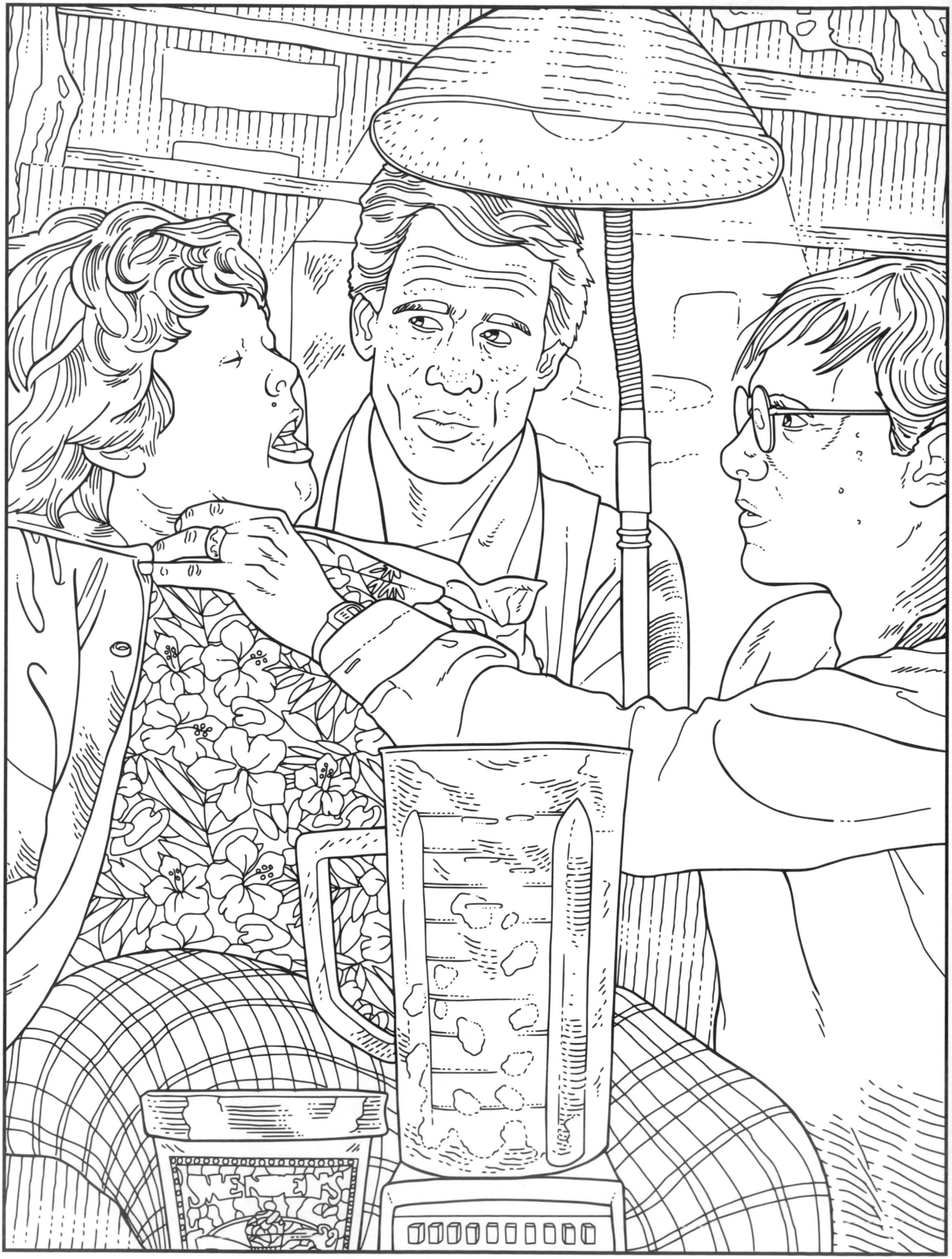

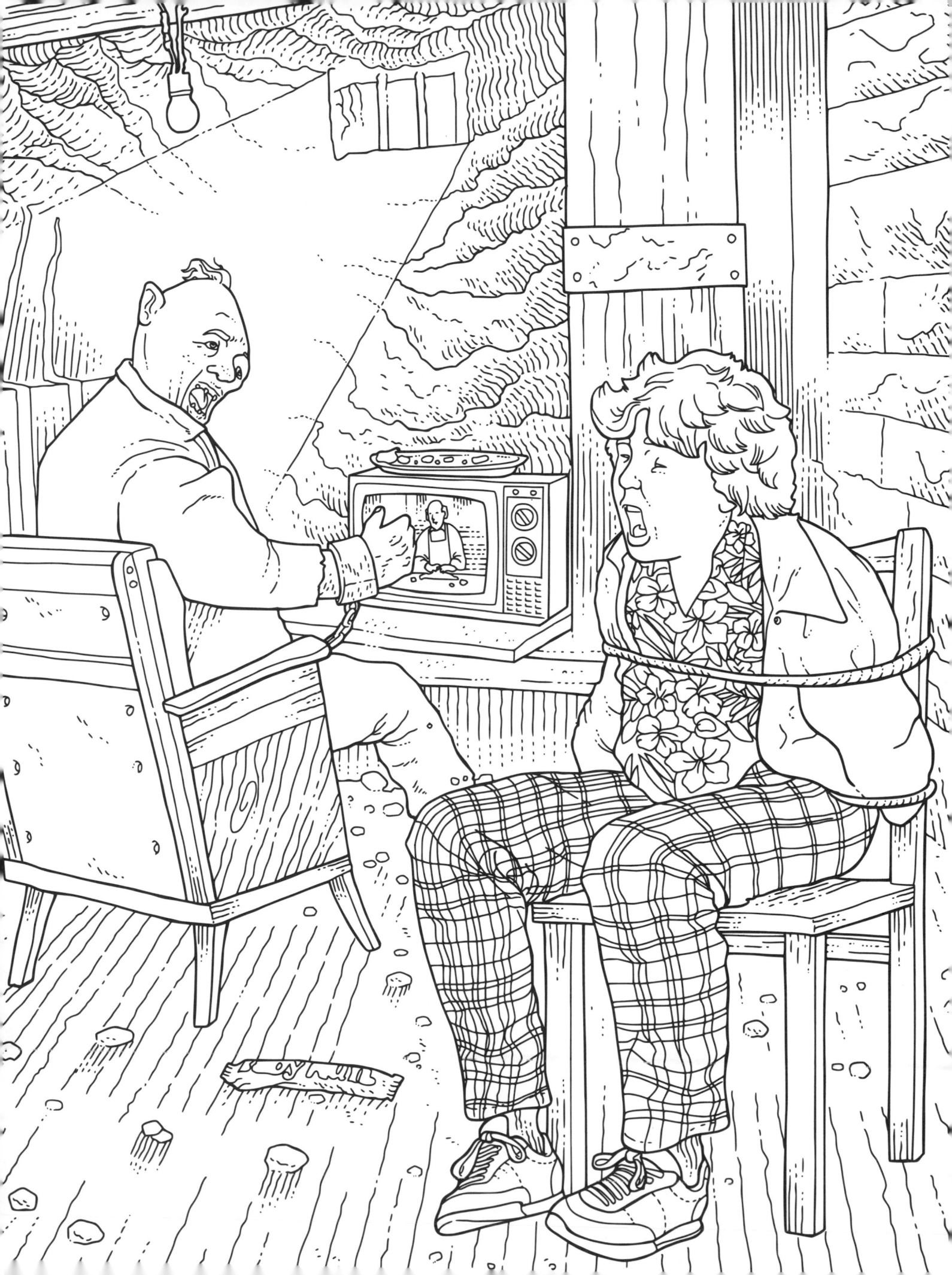

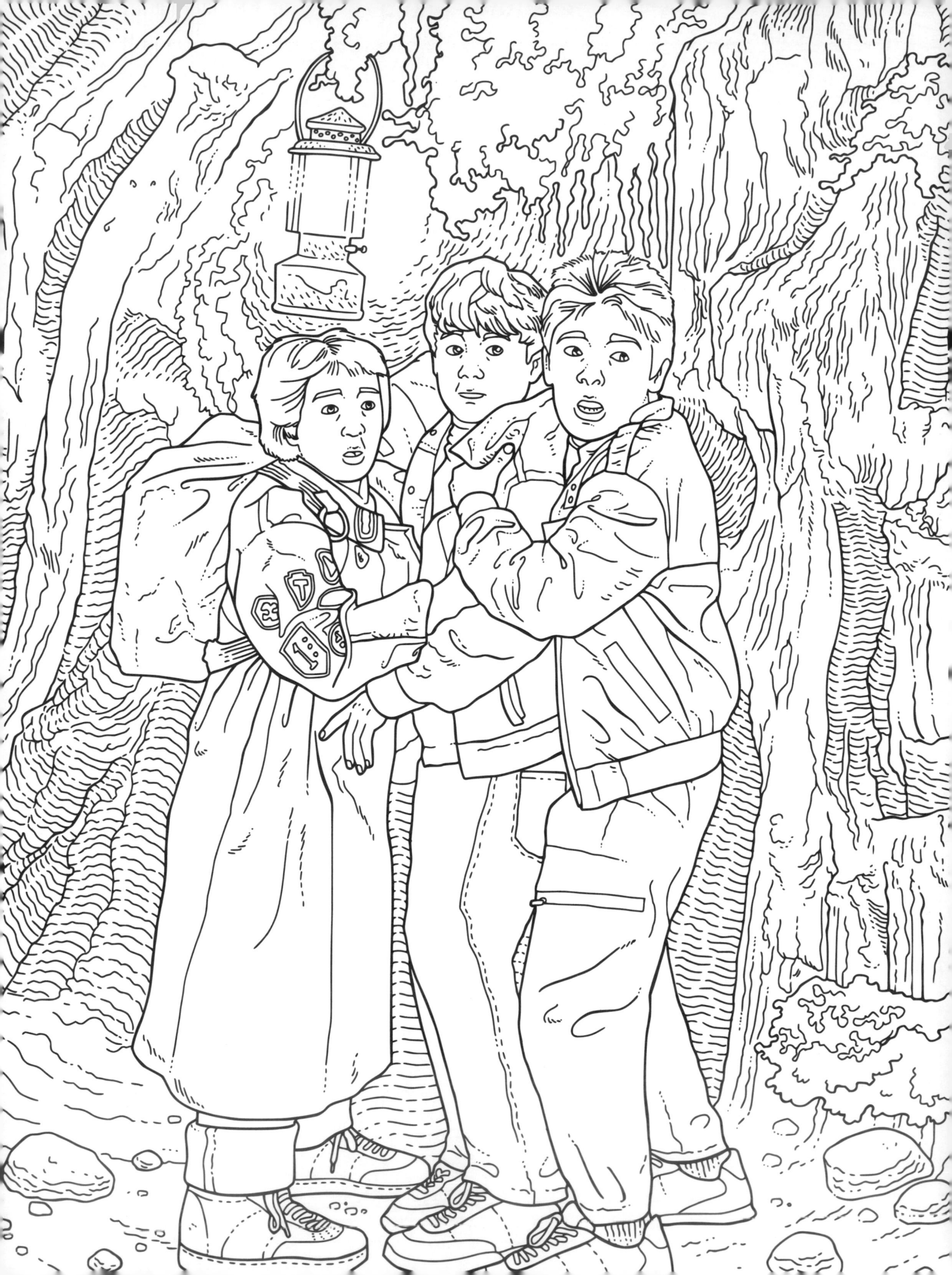

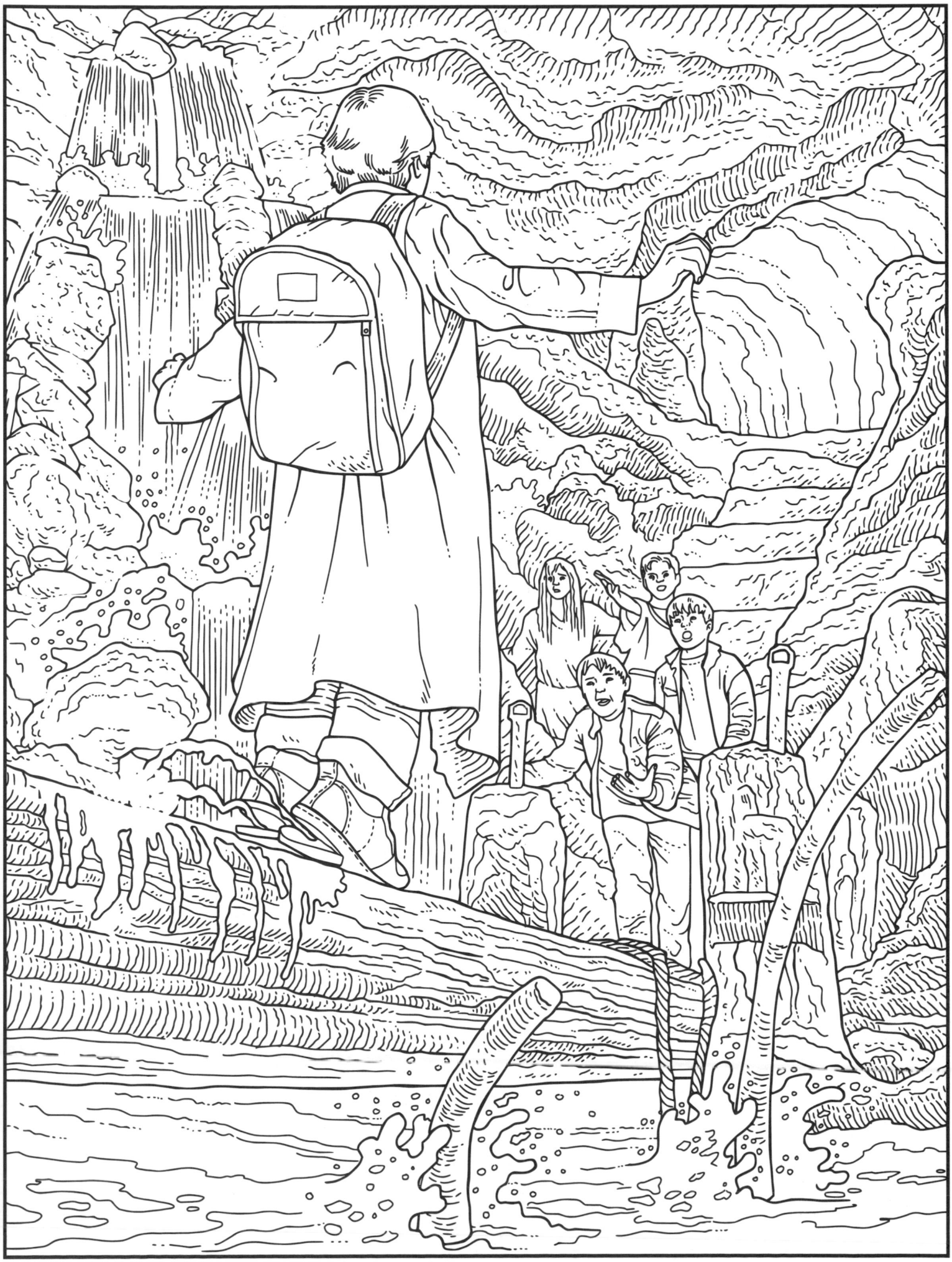

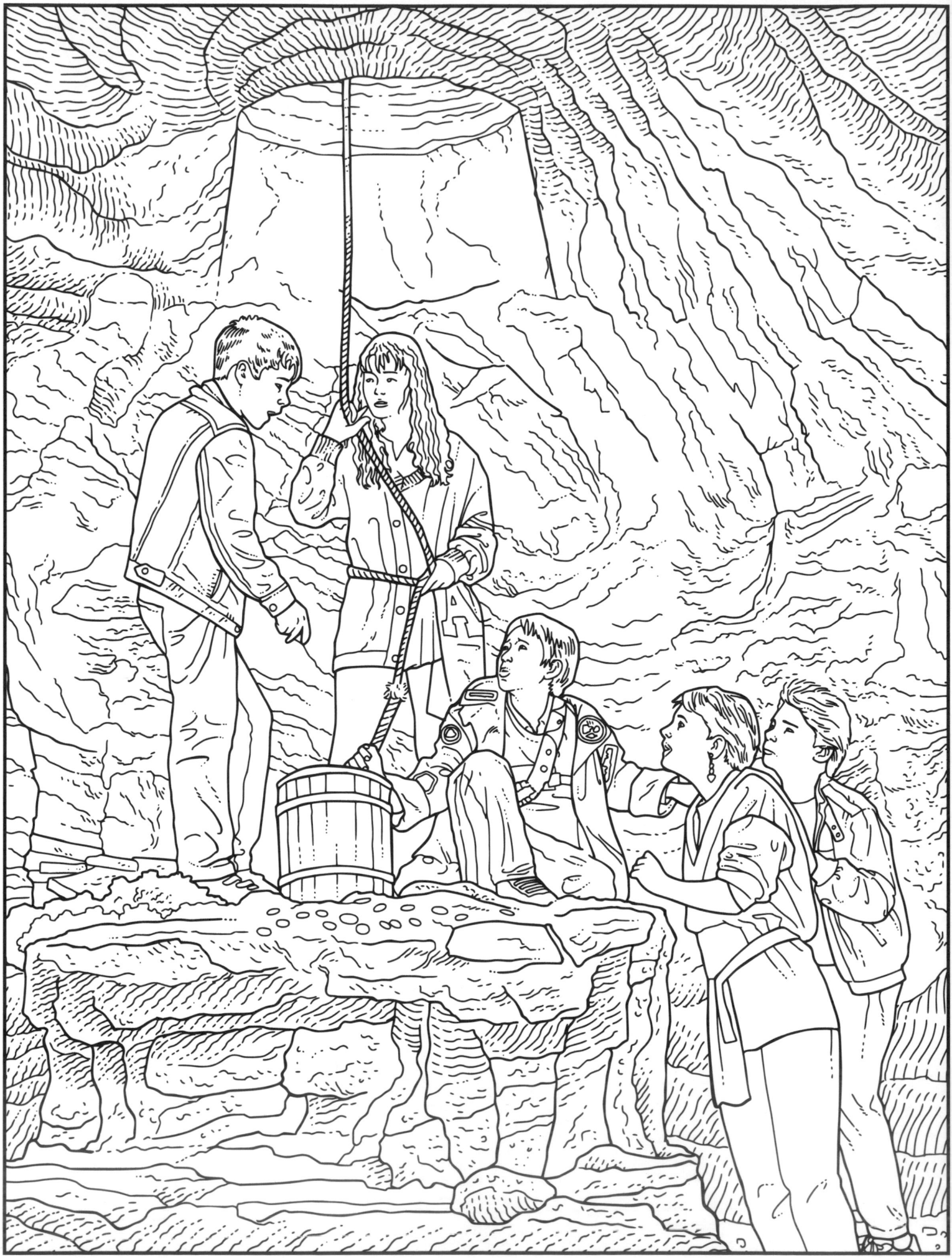

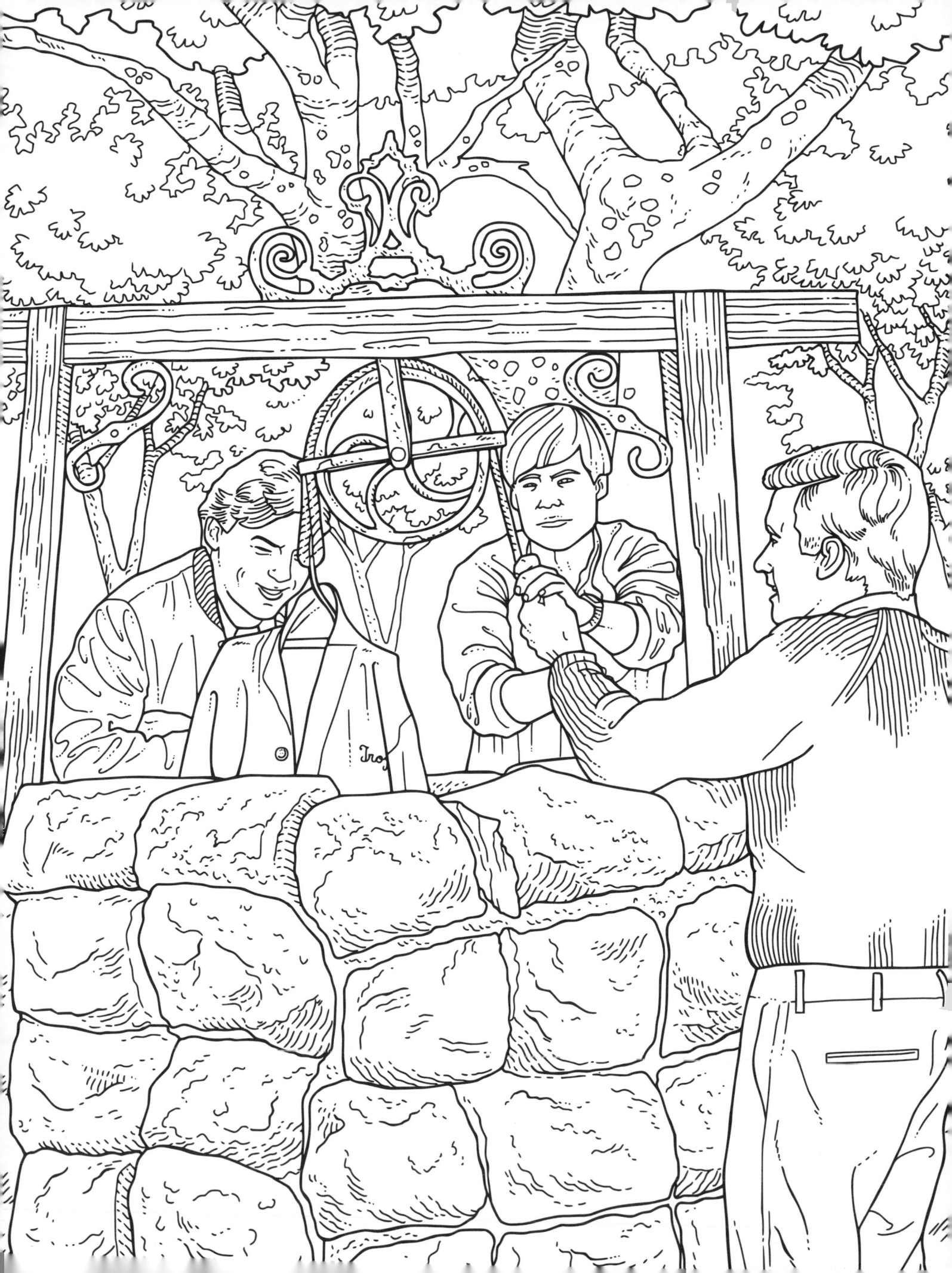

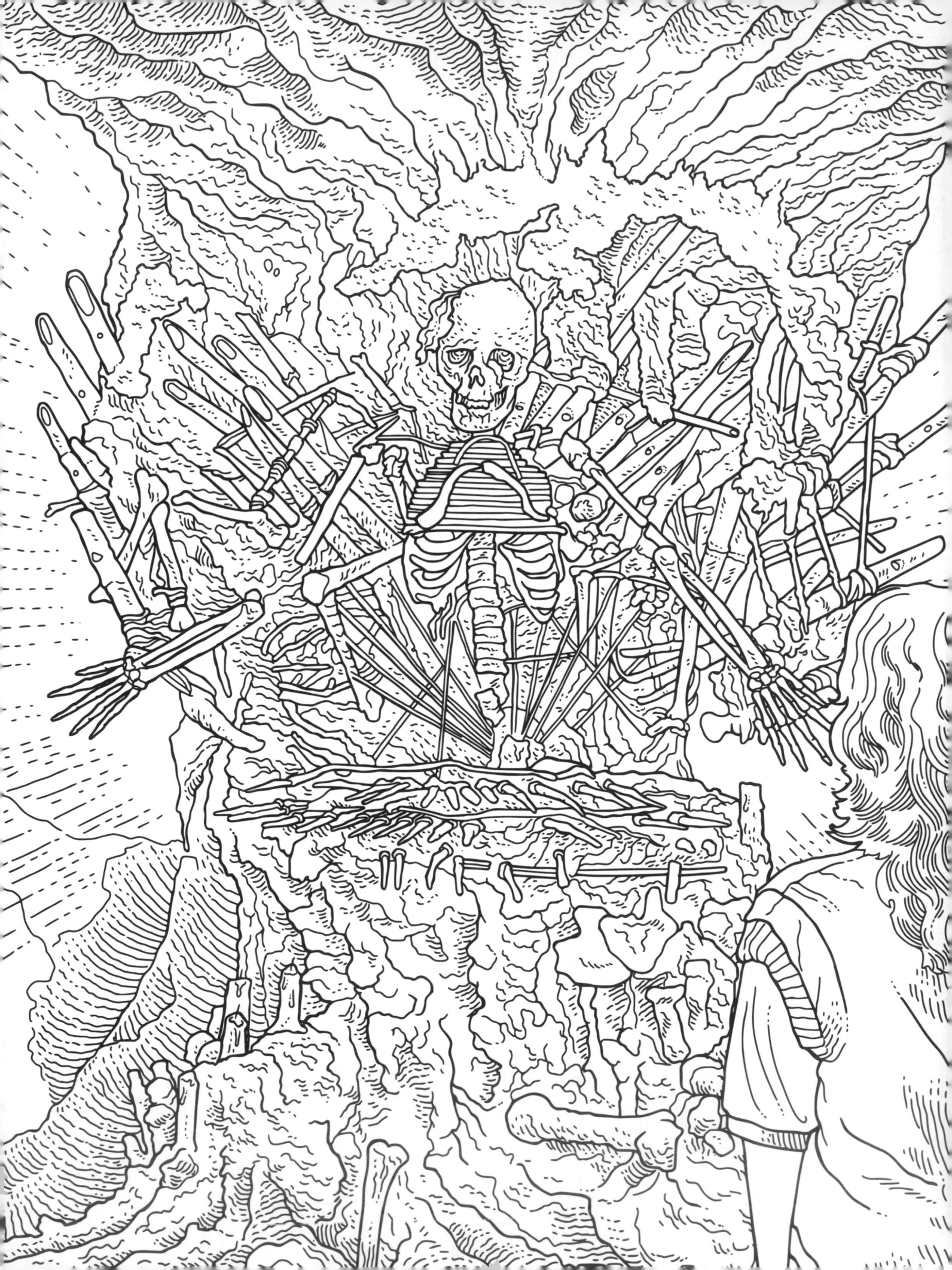

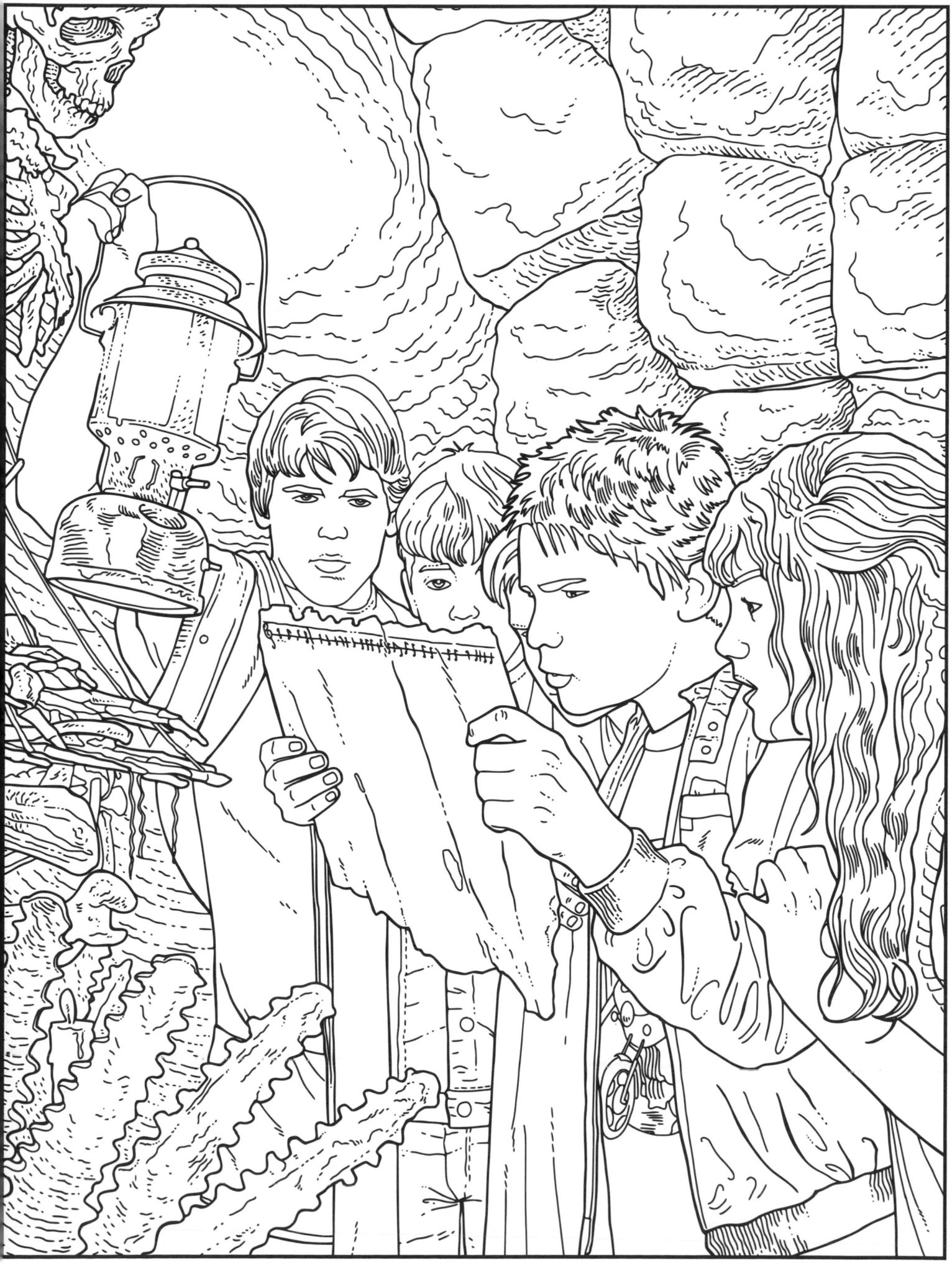

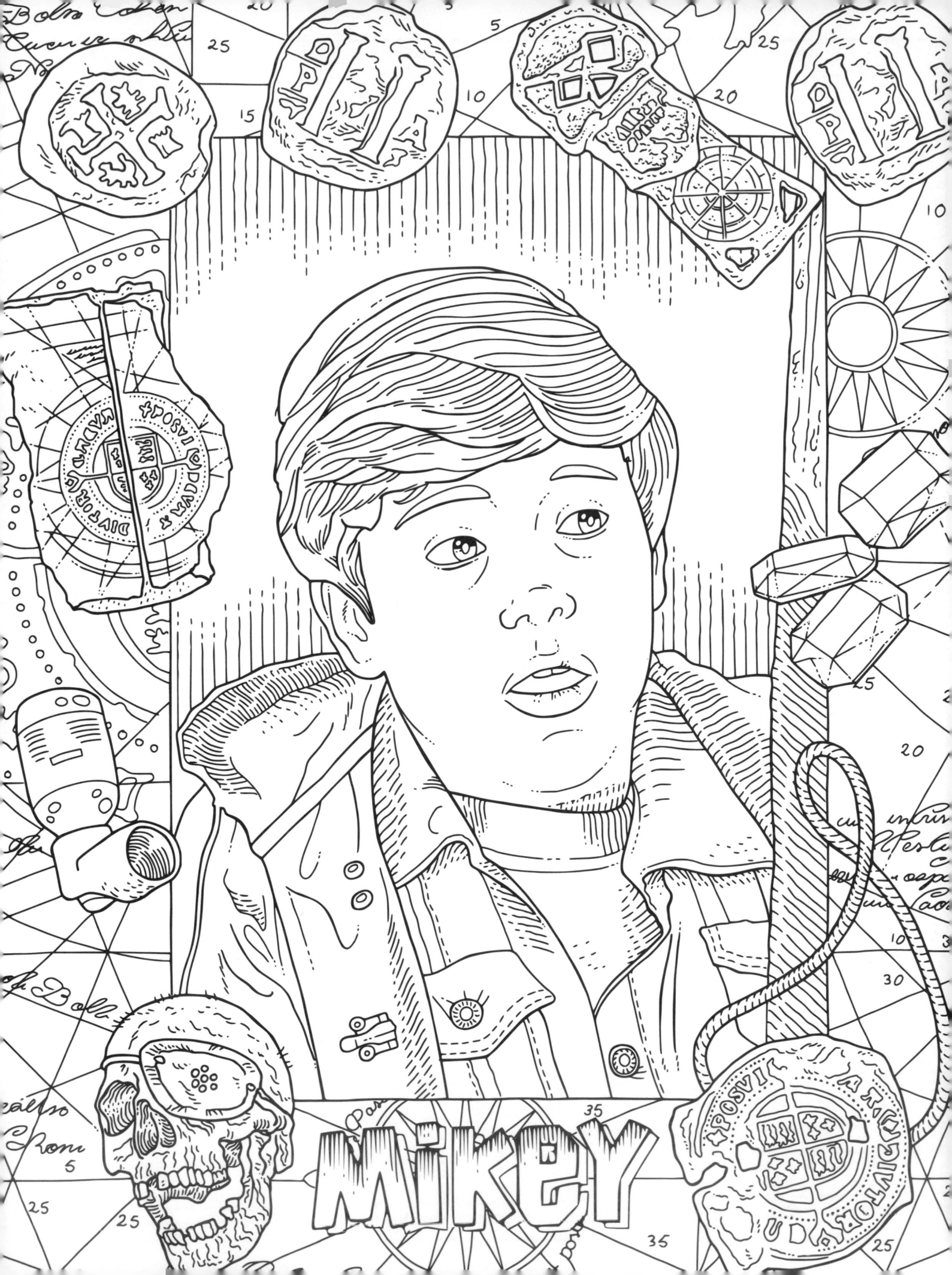
MIKEY

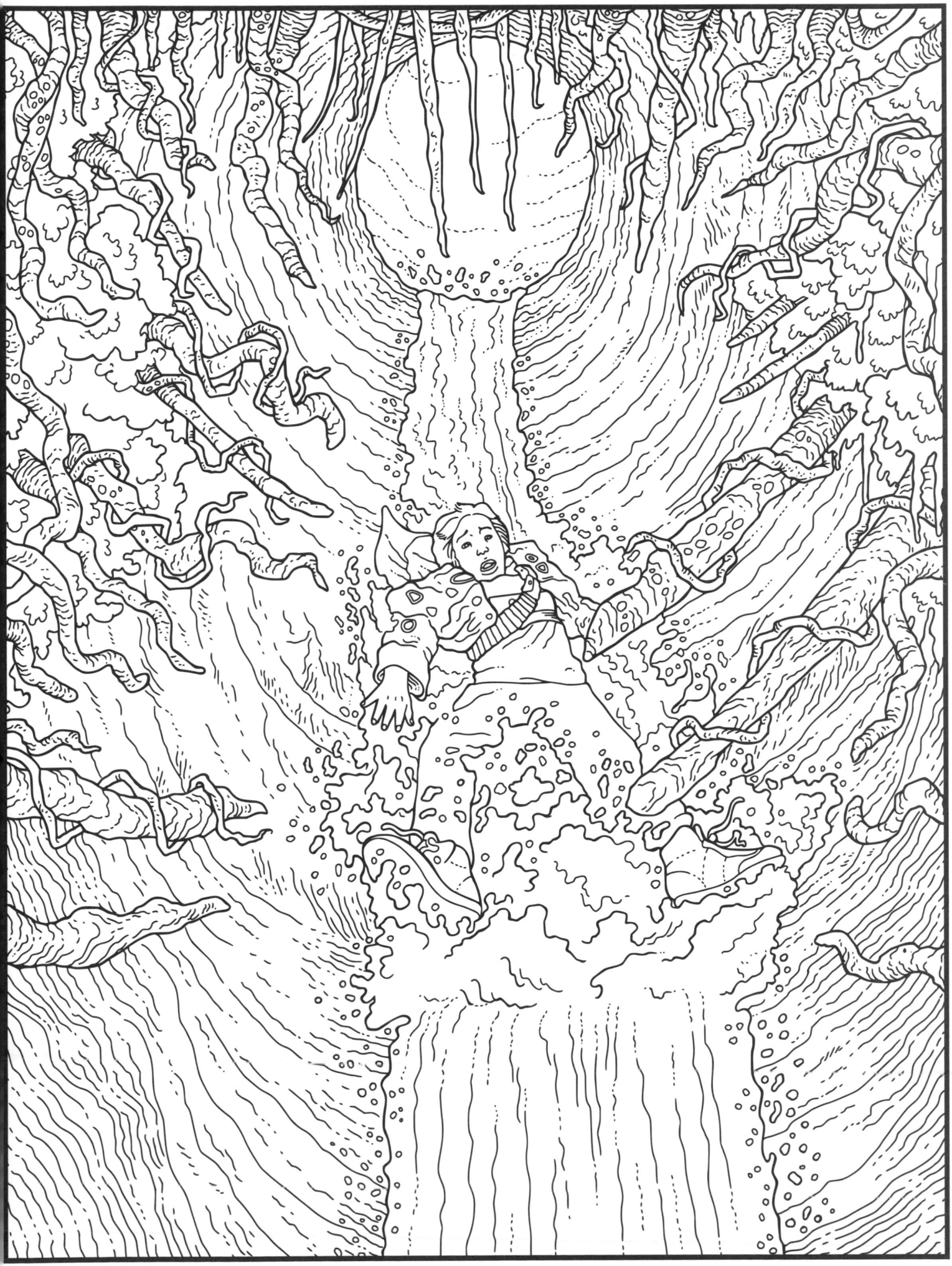

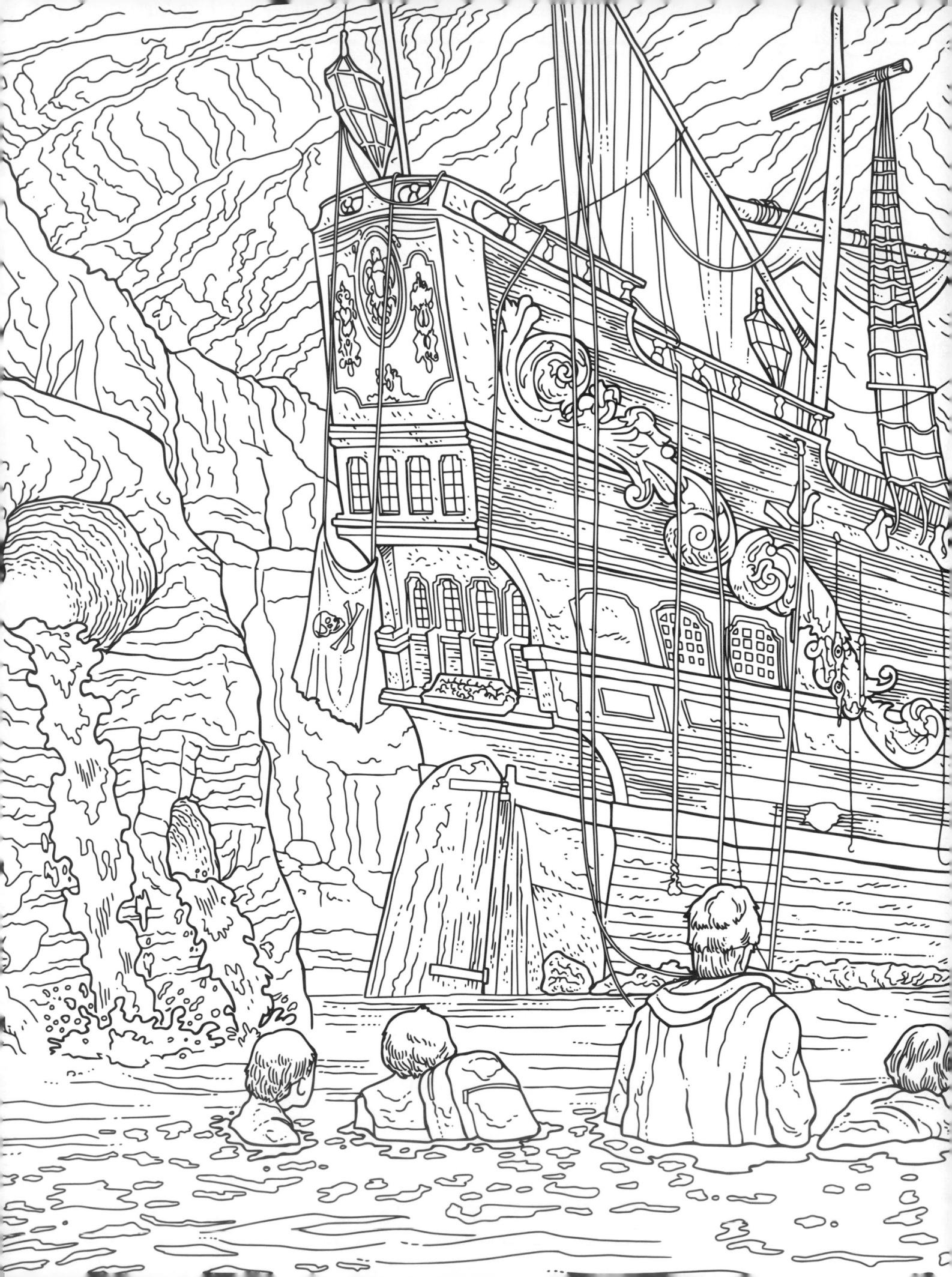

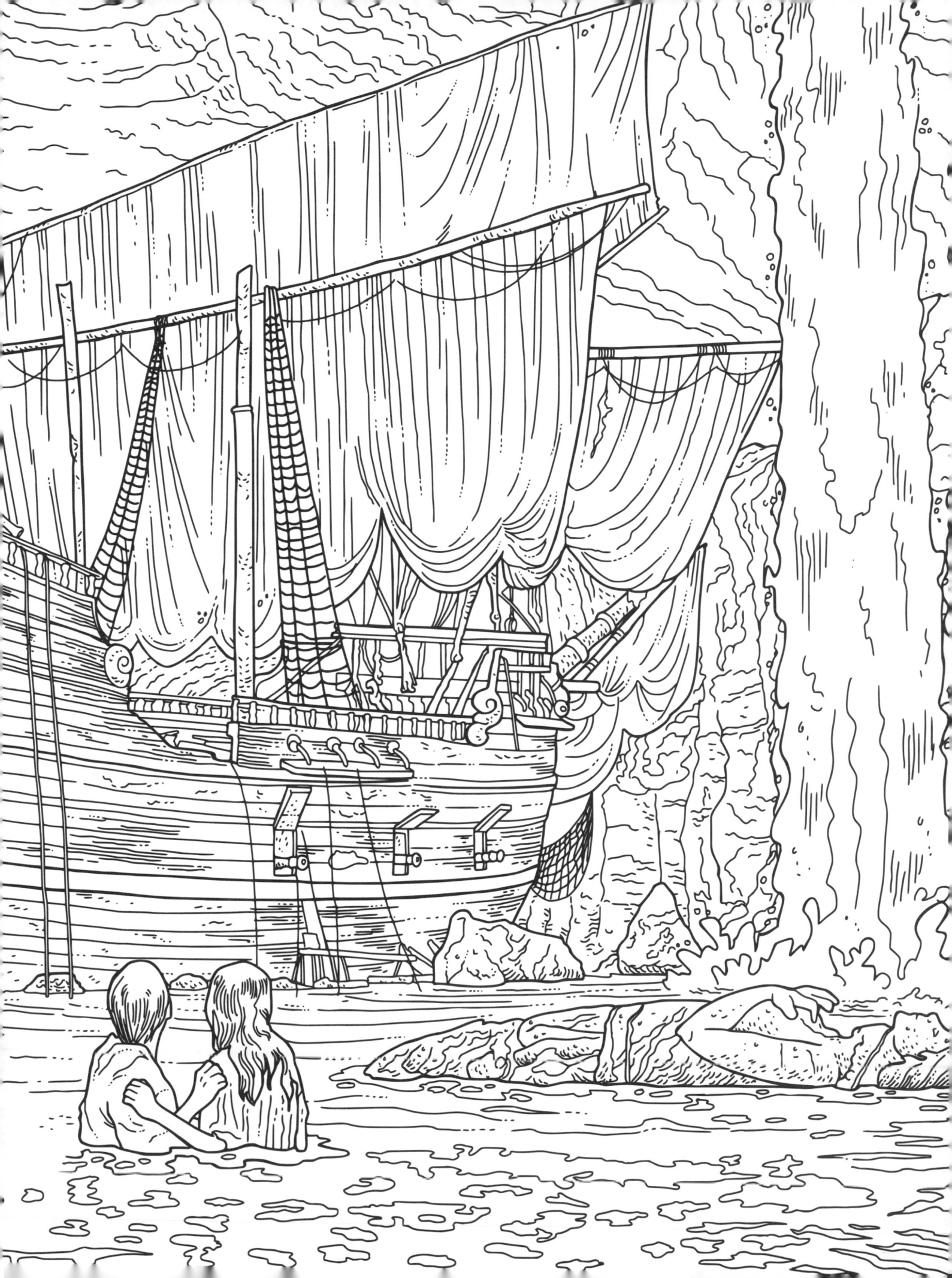

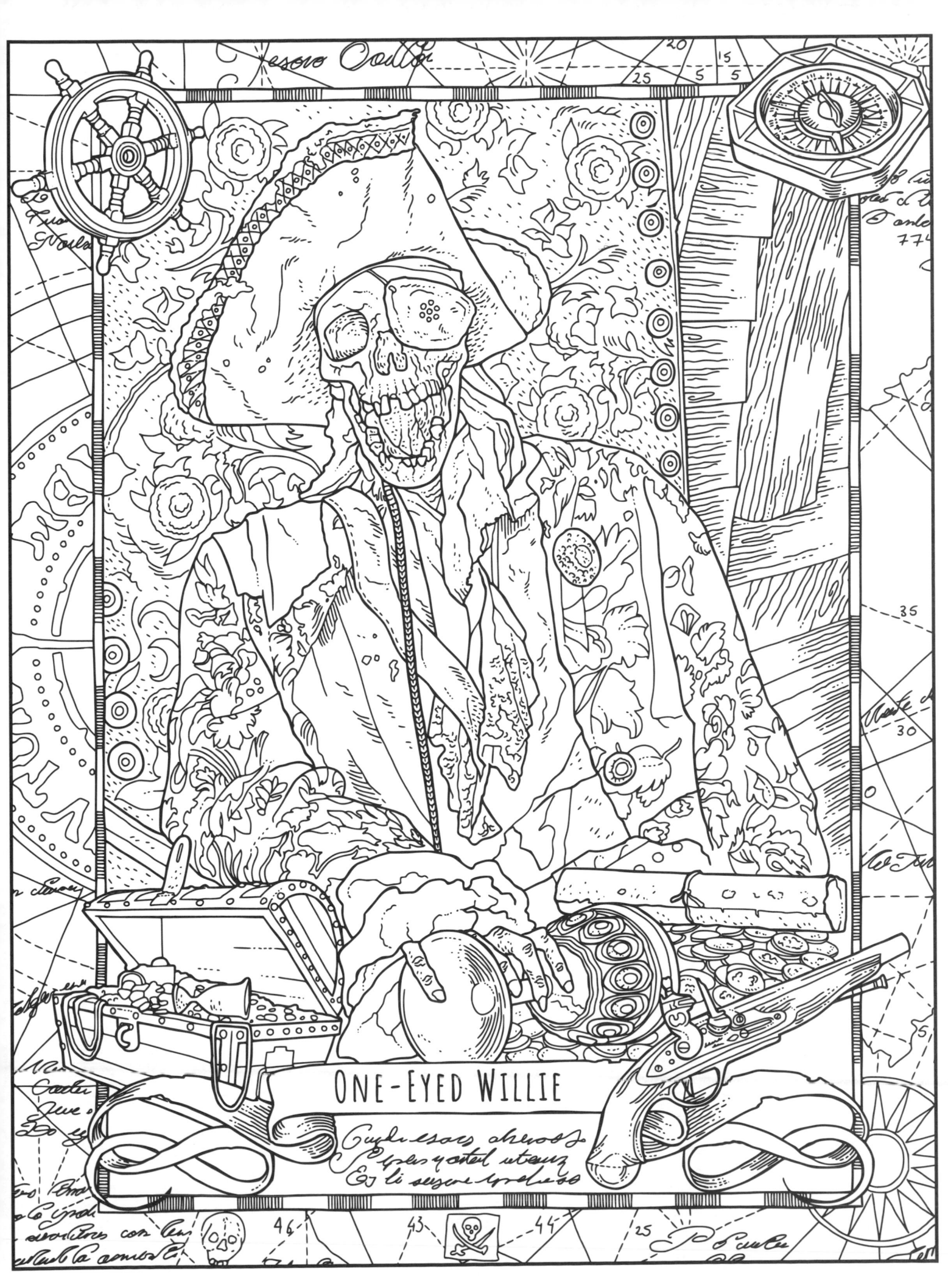
ONE-EYED WILLIE

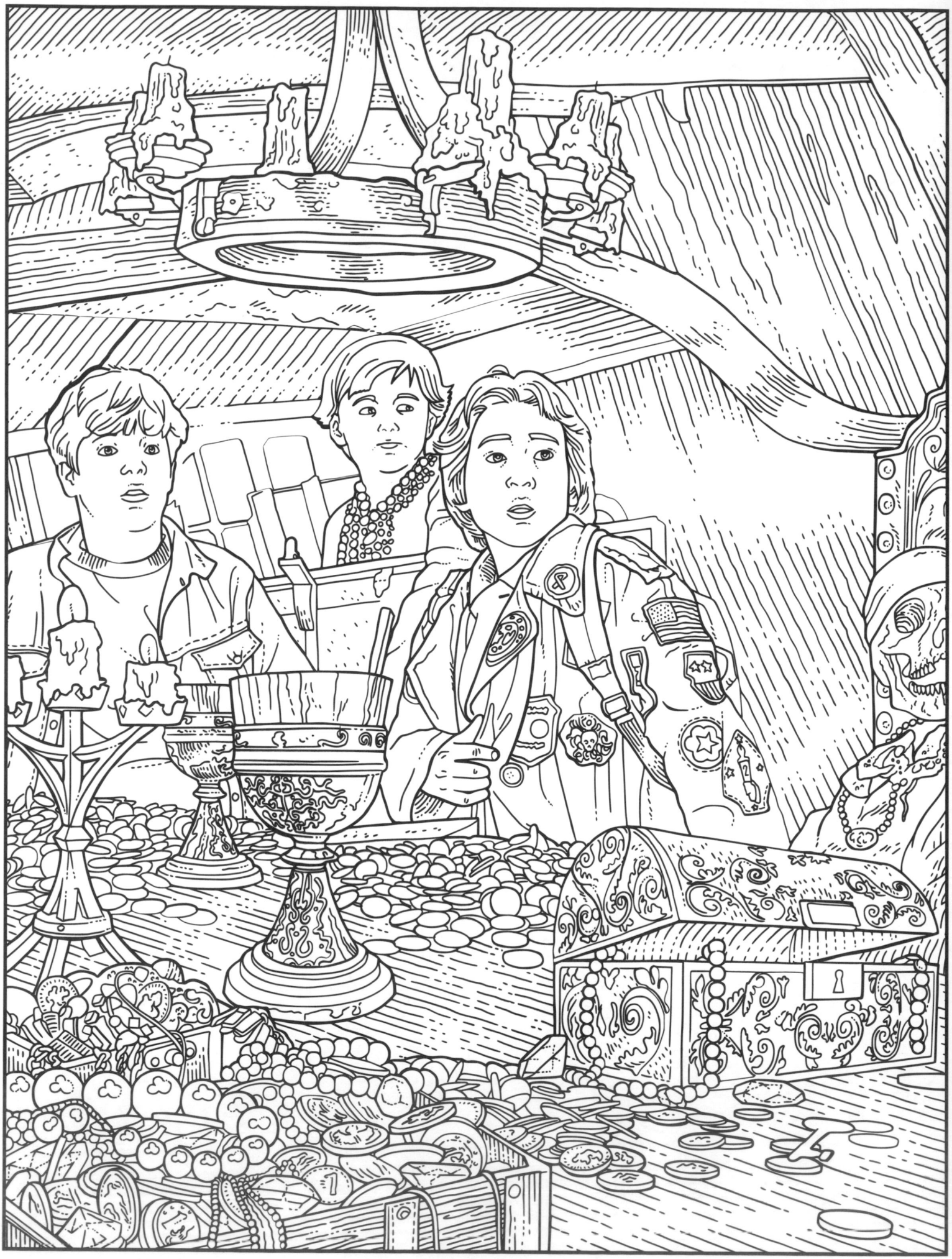

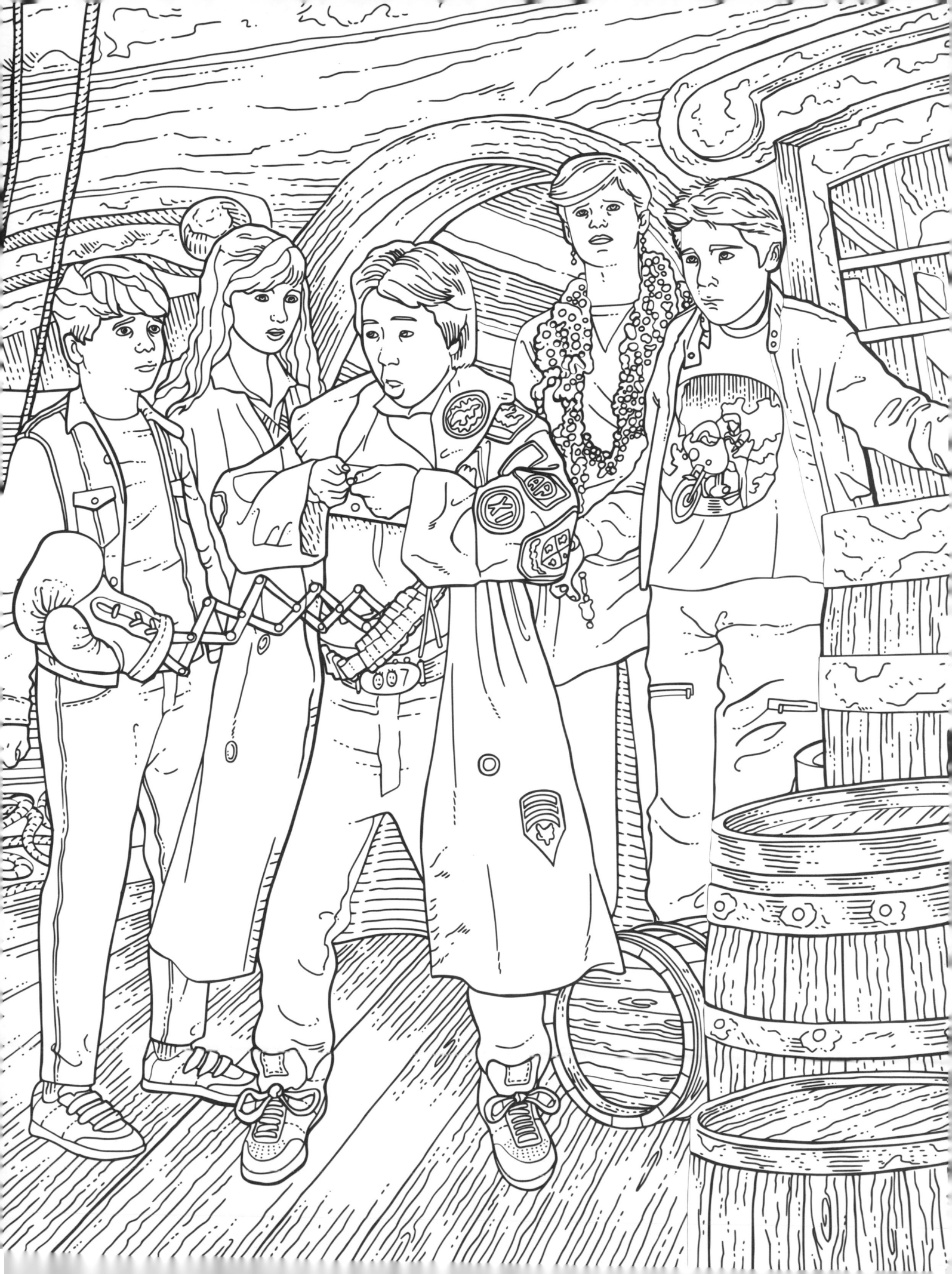
007

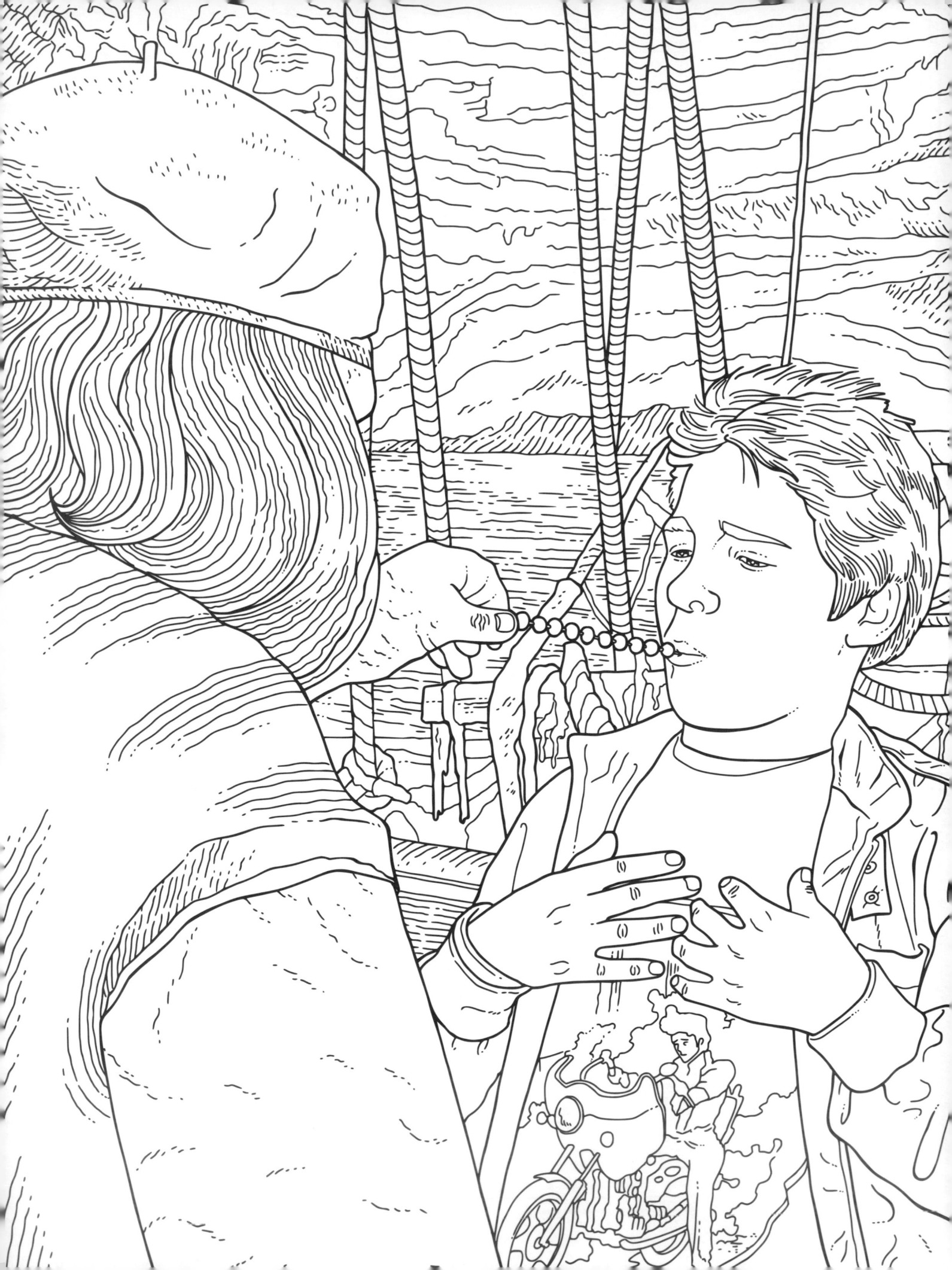

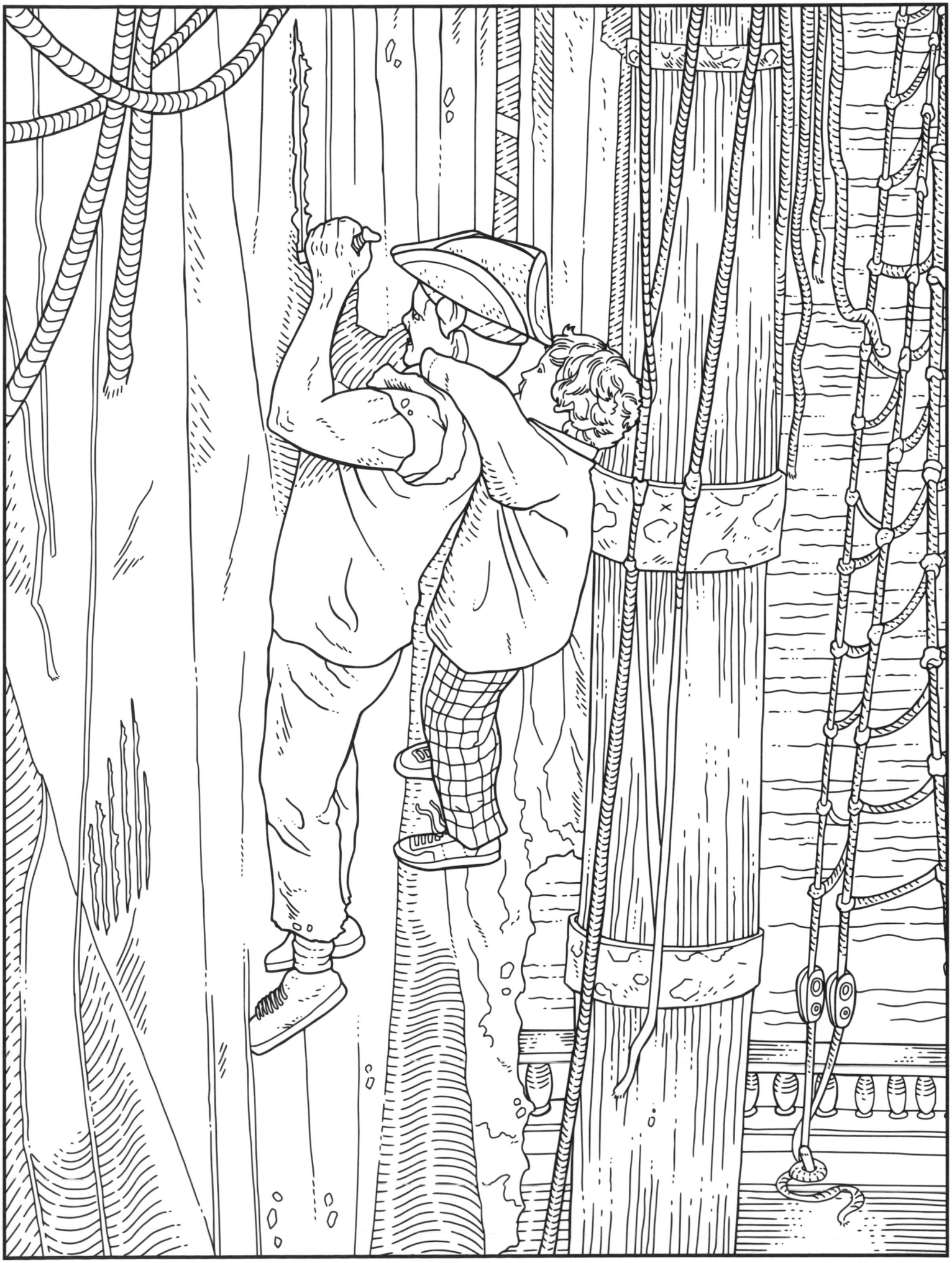

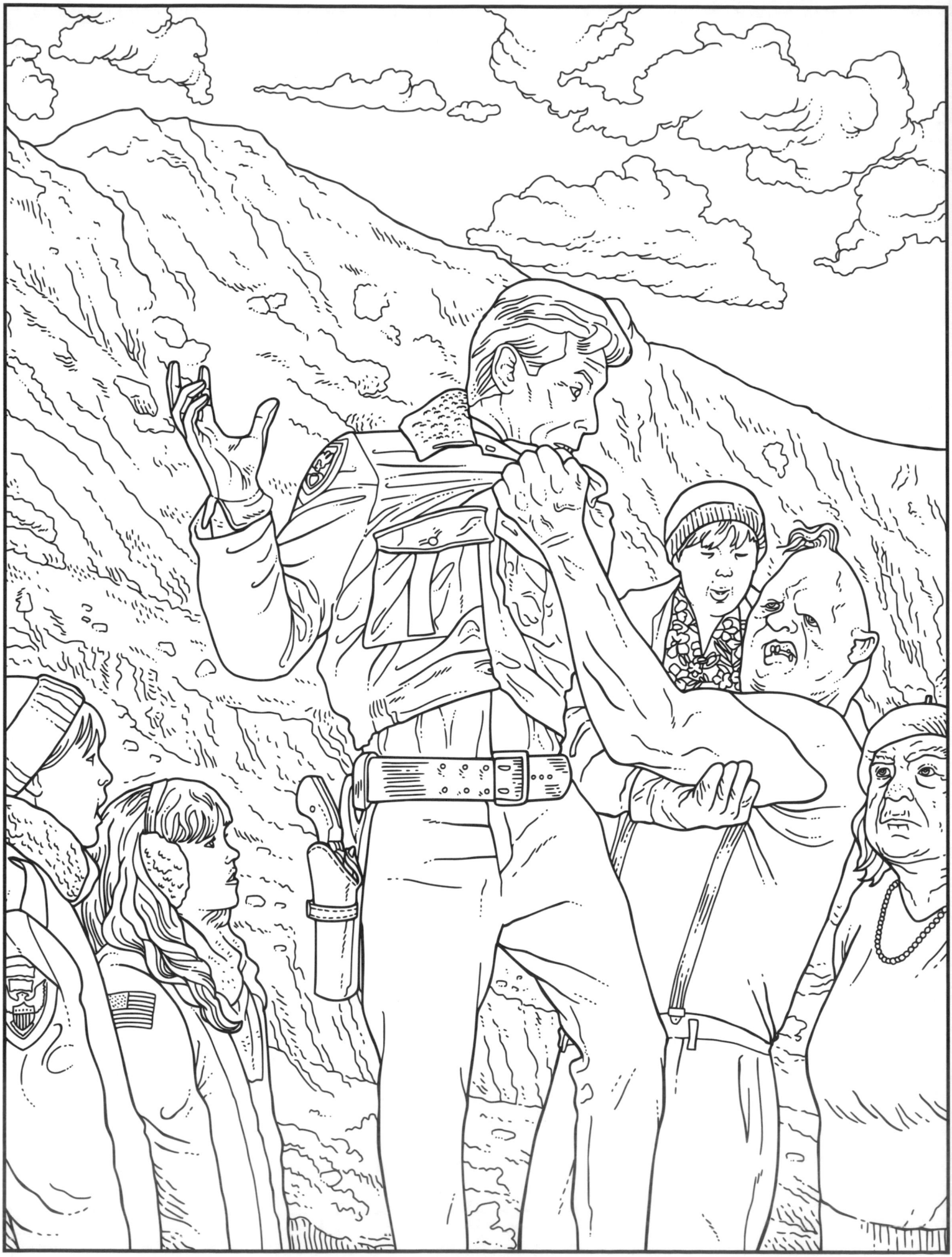

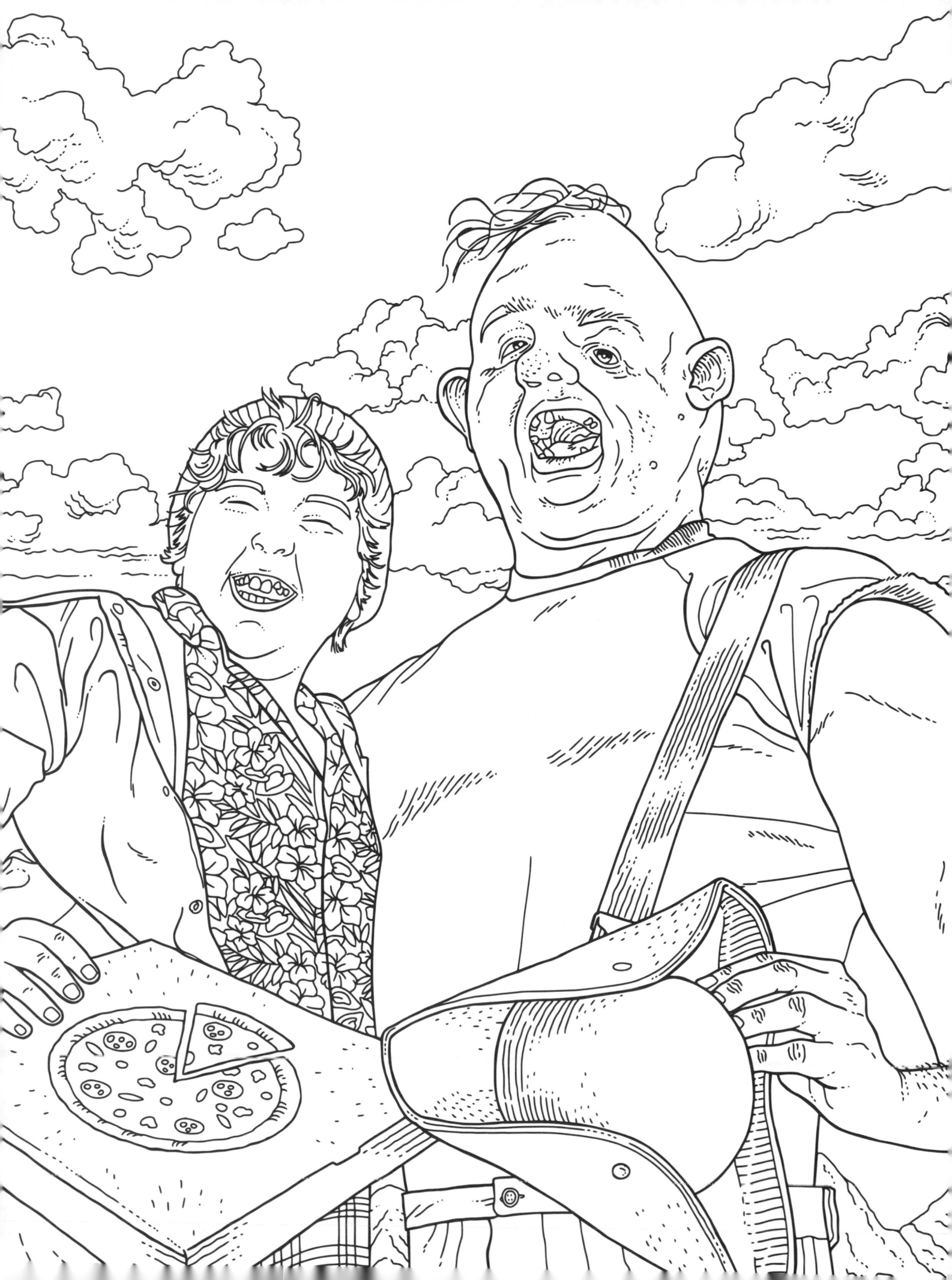

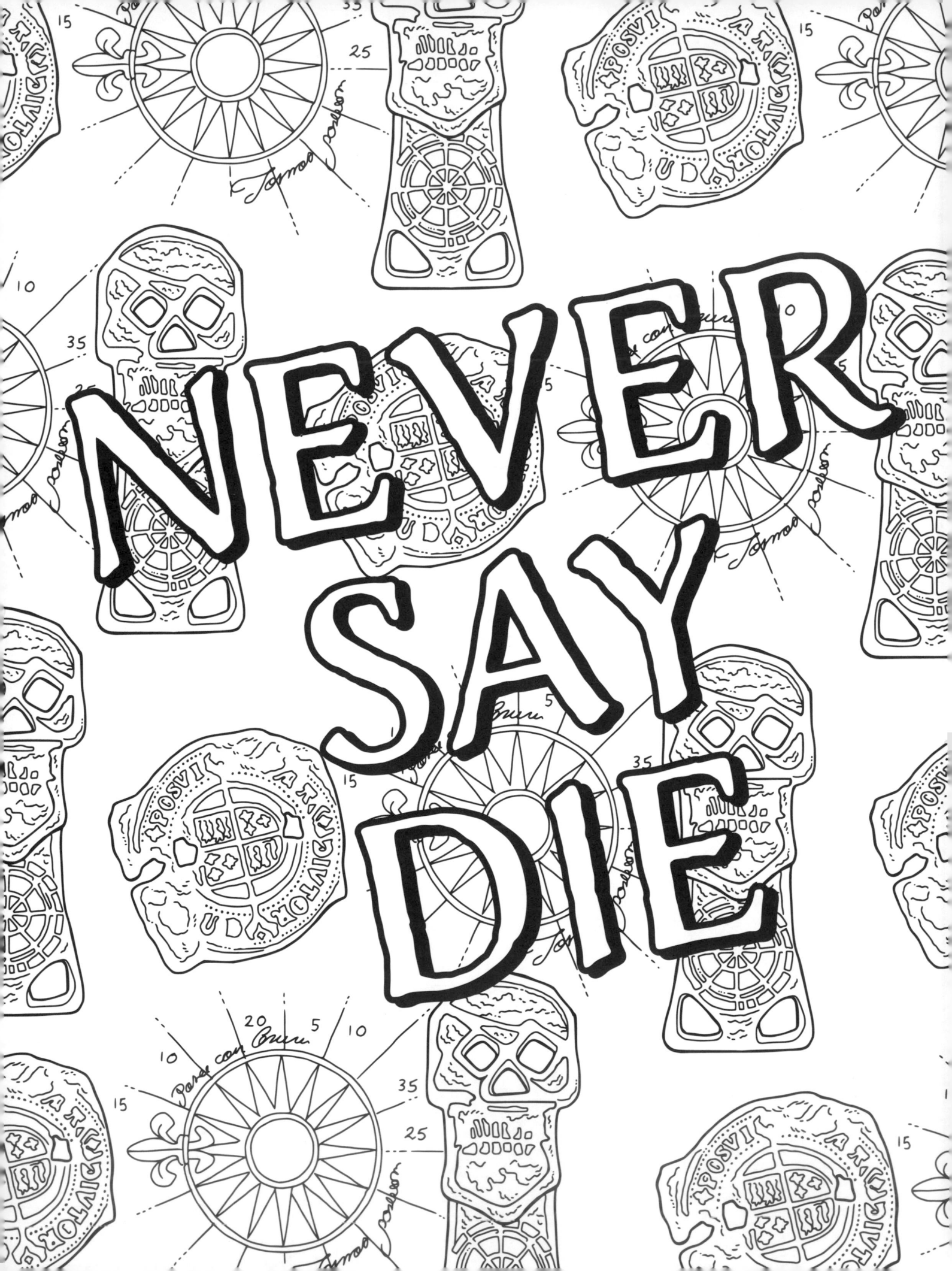
NEVER
SAY
DIE

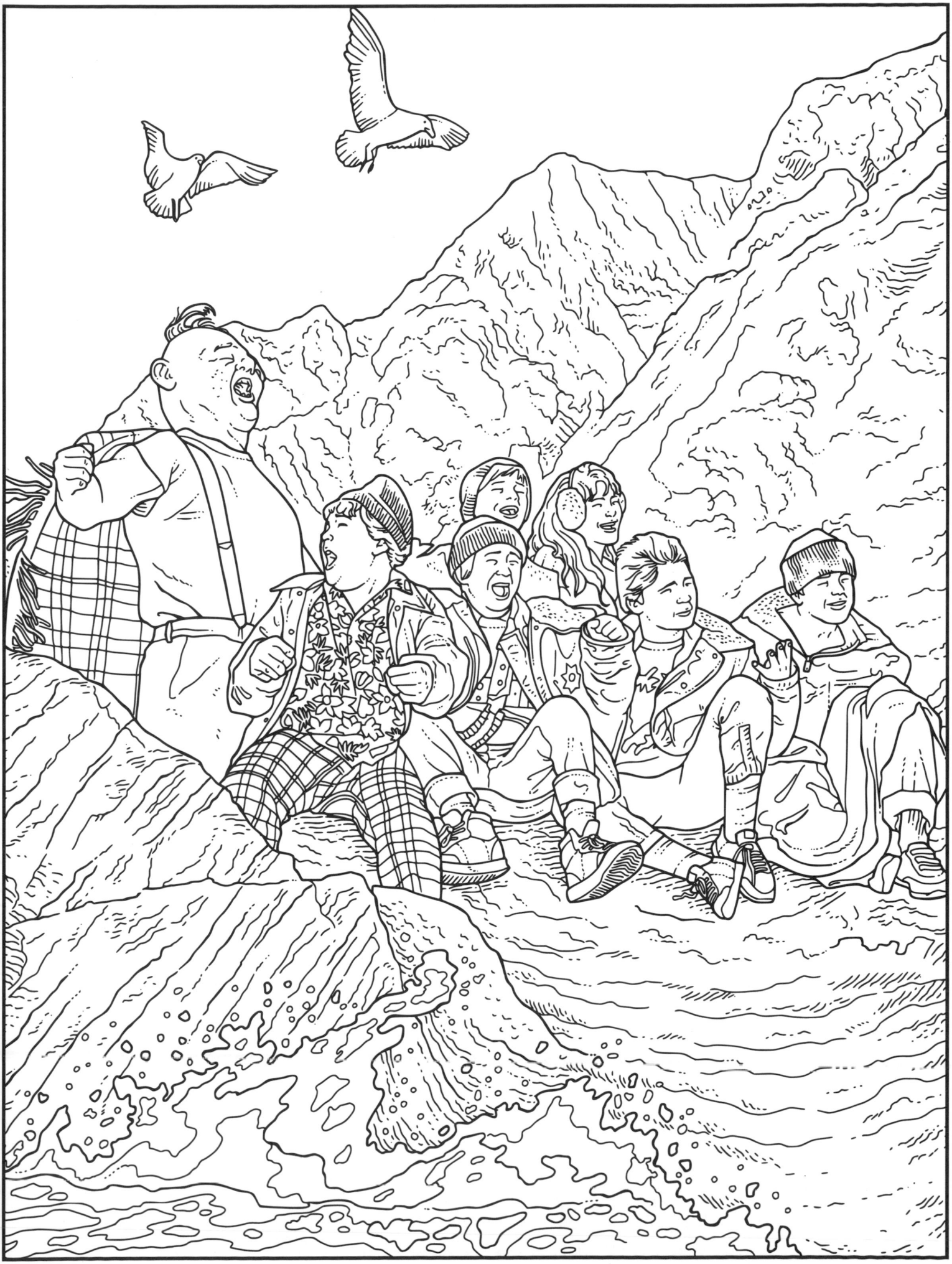

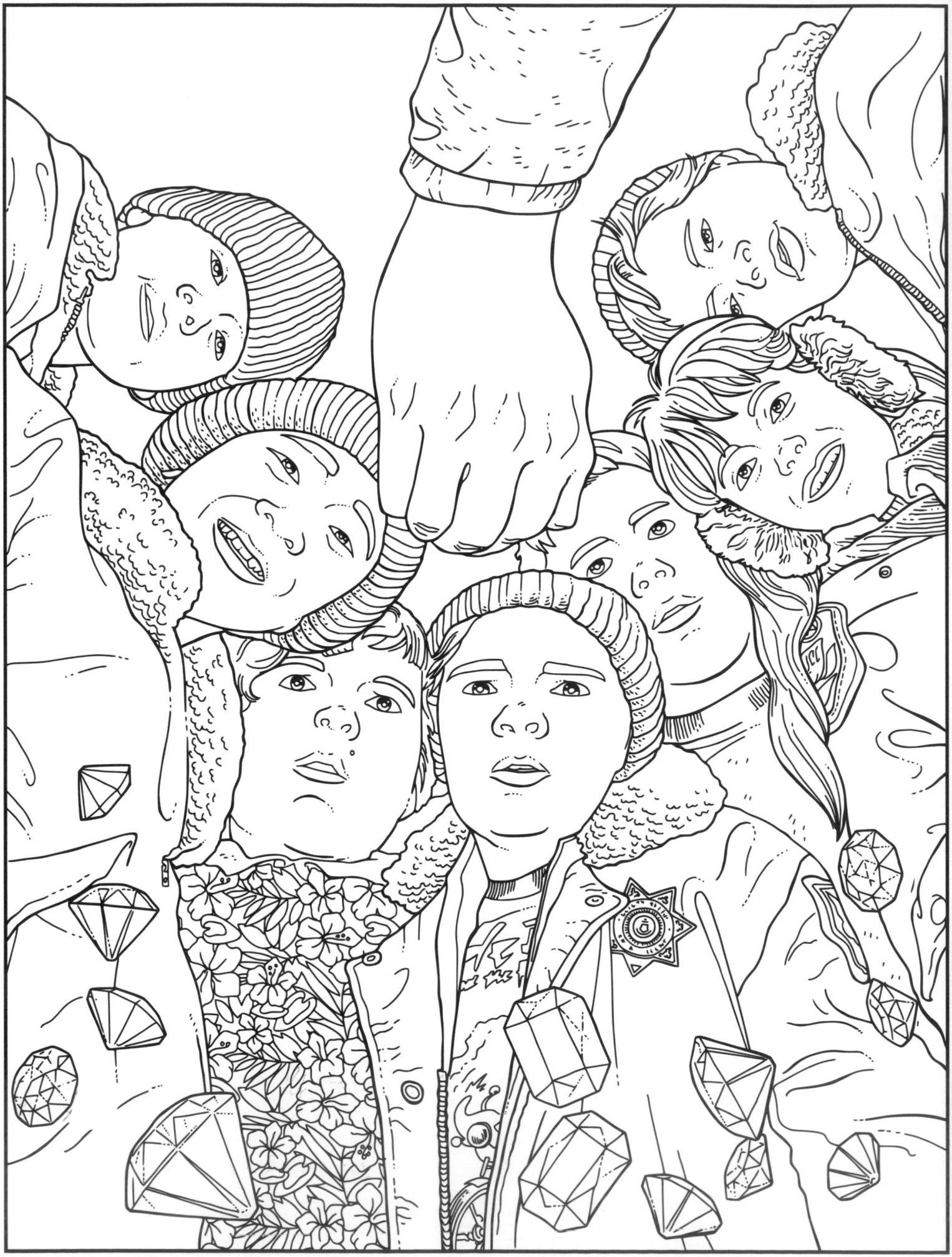

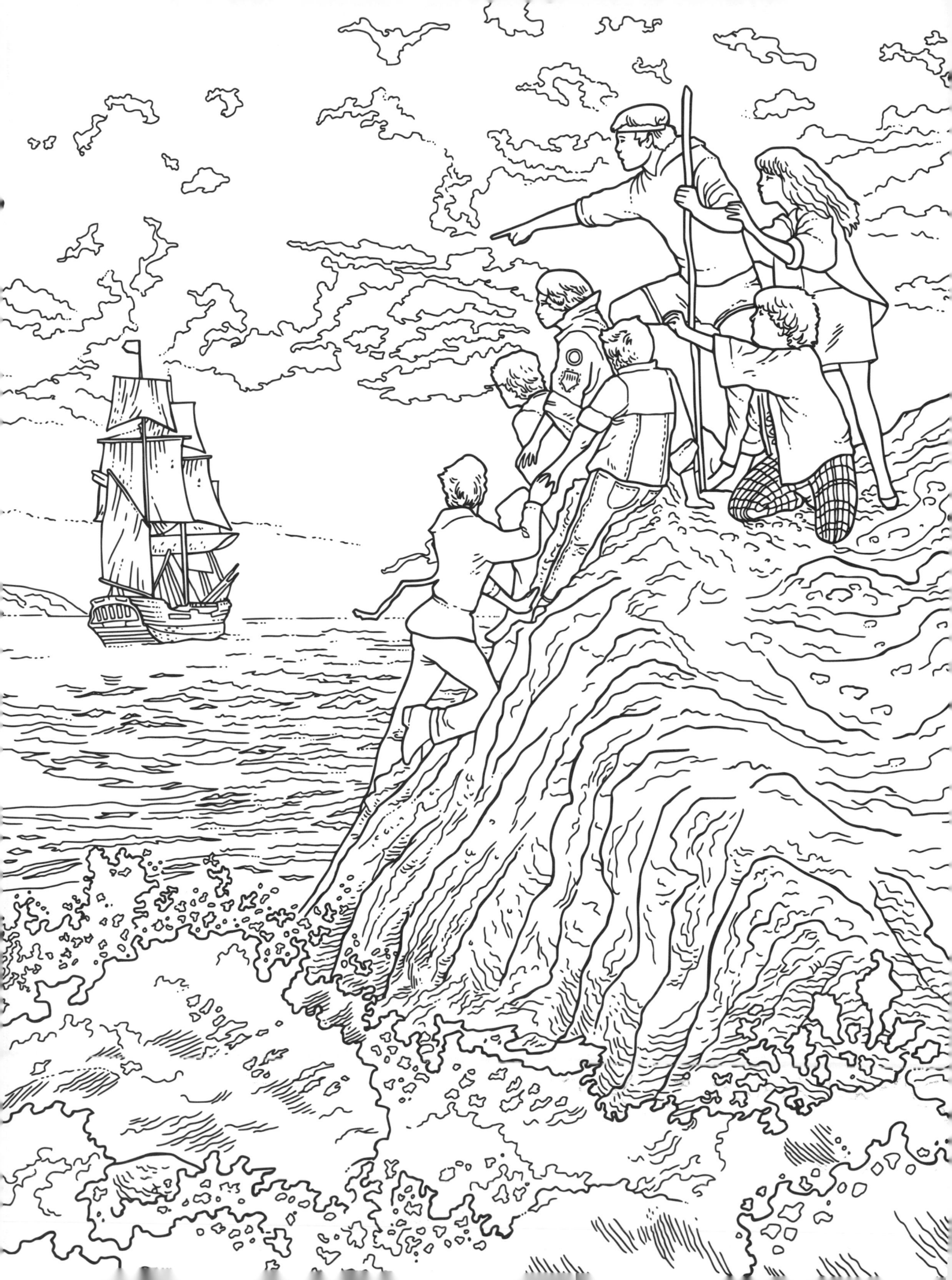

Copyright © 2022 Warner Bros. Entertainment Inc. THE GOONIES and all related characters and elements © & TM Warner Bros. Entertainment Inc. WB SHIELD: © & TM WBEI. (s22)

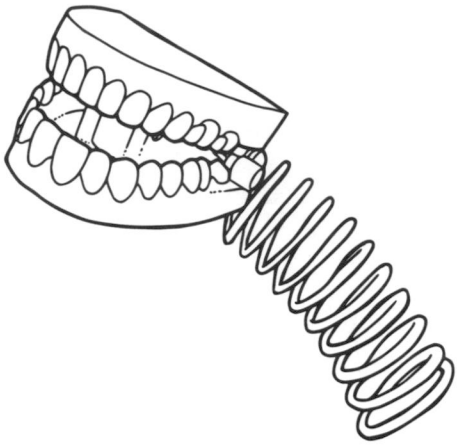

INSIGHT EDITIONS

PO Box 3088
San Rafael, CA 94912
www.insighteditions.com

Find us on Facebook: www.facebook.com/InsightEditions
Follow us on Twitter: @insighteditions

Published by Insight Editions, San Rafael, California, in 2020. All rights reserved. No part of this book may be reproduced in any form without written permission from the publisher.

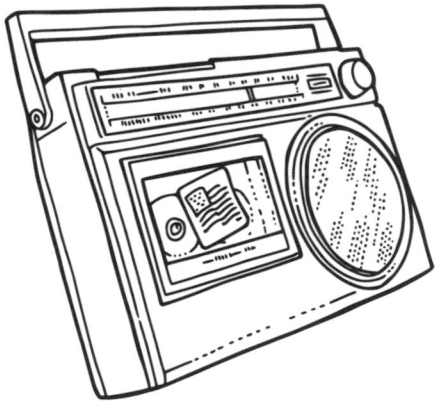

Library of Congress Cataloging-in-Publication Data available.

ISBN: 978-1-64722-196-6

Publisher: Raoul Goff
Associate Publisher: Vanessa Lopez
VP of Creative: Chrissy Kwasnik
VP of Manufacturing: Alix Nicholaeff
Associate Editor: Anna Wostenberg
Senior Production Editor: Jennifer Bentham
Senior Production Manager: Greg Steffen
Senior Designer: Judy Wiatrek Trum

Illustrations by Valentin Ramon

ROOTS of PEACE REPLANTED PAPER

Insight Editions, in association with Roots of Peace, will plant two trees for each tree used in the manufacturing of this book. Roots of Peace is an internationally renowned humanitarian organization dedicated to eradicating land mines worldwide and converting war-torn lands into productive farms and wildlife habitats. Roots of Peace will plant two million fruit and nut trees in Afghanistan and provide farmers there with the skills and support necessary for sustainable land use.

Manufactured in Turkey by Insight Editions

10 9 8 7 6 5 4 3 2 1

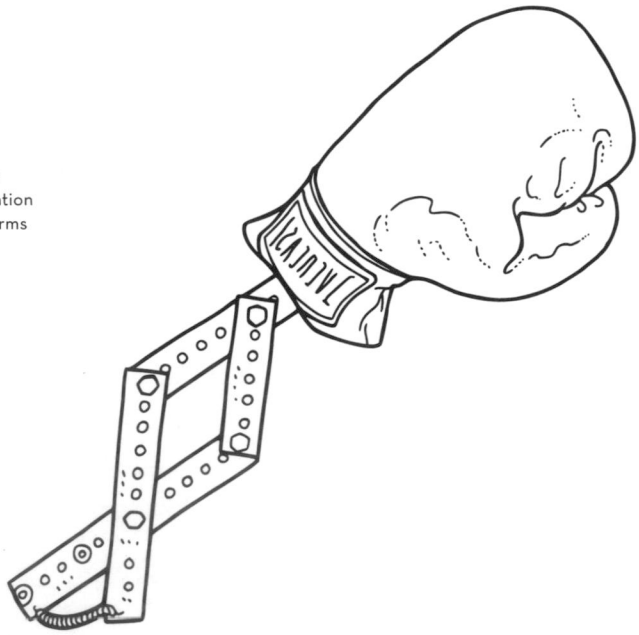